BUY BETTER CONSUME LESS

BUY BETTER CONSUME LESS

CREATE REAL ENVIRONMENTAL CHANGE

SIAN
CONWAY-WOOD

ICON

Published in the UK and USA in 2022
by Icon Books Ltd, Omnibus Business Centre,
39–41 North Road, London N7 9DP
email: info@iconbooks.com
www.iconbooks.com

Sold in the UK, Europe and Asia
by Faber & Faber Ltd, Bloomsbury House,
74–77 Great Russell Street,
London WC1B 3DA or their agents

Distributed in the UK, Europe and Asia
by Grantham Book Services, Trent Road, Grantham NG31 7XQ

Distributed in the USA
by Publishers Group West,
1700 Fourth Street, Berkeley, CA 94710

Distributed in Australia and New Zealand
by Allen & Unwin Pty Ltd,
PO Box 8500, 83 Alexander Street,
Crows Nest, NSW 2065

Distributed in South Africa
by Jonathan Ball, Office B4, The District,
41 Sir Lowry Road, Woodstock 7925

Distributed in India by Penguin Books India,
7th Floor, Infinity Tower – C, DLF Cyber City, Gurgaon 122002, Haryana

Distributed in Canada by Publishers Group Canada,
76 Stafford Street, Unit 300, Toronto, Ontario M6J 2S1

ISBN: 978-178578-811-6

Typeset in Liberation by Marie Doherty

Printed and bound in Great Britain by Clays Ltd, Elcograf S.p.A.

For Amelia Rae – who taught me
the true power of small but mighty things.

Contents

Contents

Introduction

"Open happiness"

"Start the day the happy way"

"Feel good, look good, and get more out of life"

What do these advertising slogans have in common? They all sell the idea that buying their product will make us happier, but they have something else in common too. They also all belong to some of the world's biggest brands, who are some of the planet's worst polluters, responsible for the waves of plastic waste pouring into our oceans and carbon emissions clogging up our atmosphere.

Everywhere you look, companies are trying to sell you the latest product, with advertising that promises it will make you happier, prettier or more popular, and yet the World Health Organization (WHO) estimates that around one in four people globally have at least one mental health disorder, and psychologists have found that all this consumption is actually making us miserable.[1] In the Western world we're working longer hours than ever before, buying more stuff to try to make us feel good, and getting ourselves into debt to try to keep up with the latest trends. And it's not just our personal bank balances that are overdrawn. Some of the products we buy are even produced as a result of exploitation, cause harmful pollution in their production and damage our health. Overconsuming is taking its toll on the planet. We're living in overshoot – the point at which we're using more natural resources each year than nature can regenerate. Which means we're borrowing from the future, and our ecological bank balance may soon run out.

Most of us know that advertising makes grand promises that the products we purchase usually fail to live up to. Many of us are also aware that too much shopping is bad for the planet. We even want to do something about it. So why do we find it so hard to make sustainable choices? Perhaps we should look to car manufacturer Hyundai's slogan for the answer – *Prepare to want one.* We live in a capitalist society driven by the unlimited pursuit of growth. Corporations use near-constant advertising to manipulate us into spending more, leaving it up to us to 'make the right choice' about the products we buy – without giving us all the information about how they're made or what impact they have.

We're starting to wake up to the realities of climate change, and question what we can do about it. We've realised what harm 'business as usual' is causing, and we're ready to demand change, but we're struggling to implement it. It is the wealthy CEOs and shareholders behind our fossil fuel economy who have the real power to change things – but they have no incentive to make it happen while they live lives of private luxury, built on the back of our harmful consumption habits. Whole industries, from advertising and automotive, to fashion and Big Oil, are profiting from the status quo, as long as we continue to purchase – which is why they're investing billions in covering up the truth about the climate crisis to keep us spending.

They want us to think there's nothing we can do about it, which is why they carefully control the narratives around climate change in our shops, on our screens and even in the way our countries are run. But increasingly around the world, people are taking back their power, escaping the stronghold of polluting corporations and demanding change. And now it's your turn.

Chances are, if you've picked up this book, you've already had that 'lightbulb moment' inspiring you to reduce your impact on the planet. For many of us, it starts with something shocking. Upsetting footage of a whale grieving her dead calf killed by plastic pollution, worry over wildfires destroying homes and animal habitats, or heartbreaking images of orangutans trying to fend off the bulldozers tearing down their rainforest homes. Seeing our favourite species pushed to the brink of extinction, noticing litter mounting up on the kerbs in our local neighbourhoods or even looking out the window at 'freak' weather events that are becoming our new normal.

For me, it began with a pair of trousers. On holiday in Cambodia in 2015, I'd spent the day with local artisans, learning about the skill and effort that goes into traditional silk weaving, and admiring the beautiful fabrics they were creating. That night, as I got ready for bed, I noticed that the trousers I'd been wearing, purchased cheaply from a high-street retailer in the UK, said 'Made in Cambodia' on the label. Having seen the time and skill it took to weave fabric by hand, I began to wonder, like many ethical fashion activists before me, 'who made my clothes?' And if I'd only paid £10 for them, how much did the person making them get paid?

When I got home, I fell down an ethical-fashion rabbit hole, learning about the horrors of modern slavery, exploitation and environmental destruction behind the fashion industry and the cheap clothes I had been, until then, enjoying. As a marketer in my day job, I began to see how people like me were using our skills to sell cheap products that people didn't really need, at a true cost to workers in supply chains and the planet we all share. What started as a mission to clean up my wardrobe eventually turned into a reframe of my entire relationship with consumption. Along the way, I blogged about the things I was learning, and began connecting with other like-minded ethical consumers online. As I met small business owners who were doing all that they could to make their products ethically and sustainably, I witnessed how much they were struggling to compete against big brands with huge advertising budgets, and I knew I could help.

A single 'made in' label led me on a journey of lifestyle changes, new connections and a complete career change, as I left the corporate world behind in 2017 to work with ethical and sustainable small businesses. I started the #EthicalHour community as a Twitter chat, founded on the idea that if we could all dedicate just one hour a week to learning more about ethics, sustainability and how to buy better, we could begin to make improvements without getting overwhelmed. As the network grew, I began teaching small businesses how to be more sustainable and market themselves ethically, drawing together a whole community of people who believe profit shouldn't come at the expense of people and planet. Today #EthicalHour connects over 61,000 people worldwide (growing every day!), united in our mission to create a world where business is a force for good.

But back to Ethical Hour's early days, and the start of my journey into sustainable living. I was proud to consider myself a 'conscious consumer'. I spent hours researching brands and carefully considering my purchases. Bamboo coffee flask in hand, I switched to a renewable energy provider at home and sent my friends a referral code to encourage them to do the same. When I signed up for a recycled toilet paper subscription, I proudly shared their discount scheme. I promoted the plant-based meal box I signed up to, and got some free meals when my mum joined too. The more I talked about them, the more my small swaps spread through my social circles and online audience – a ripple effect of positive actions that made me think, *surely, if enough people cared about the planet, and knew these options existed, we wouldn't be in such a mess?*

Since 2017, it has felt like that ripple has become a wave. In the UK, the *Blue Planet II* documentary brought the reality of plastic pollution into our homes and the tide began to turn overnight. Suddenly everyone seemed to carry reusables. Brands made big pledges about their plastic waste in response to public pressure. Zero-waste shops started popping up on high streets across the country, single-use items like plastic cotton buds were banned and it was slightly easier to find *some* plastic-free produce in the supermarkets. Since then, in cities around the world, Extinction Rebellion have brought 'business as usual' to a halt with their civil disobedience, students have been on climate strike, and governments and corporations have begun to declare a climate emergency. Finally, climate change has become a mainstream topic in conversation, beyond the usual echo chamber of concerned environmentalists.

Yet every week I notice my household waste and recycling is still overflowing, and I'm not alone. Deliveries still arrive in mountains of plastic wrap, and finding good quality alternatives to everything isn't always easy or convenient. After the initial awareness wore off, lots of people began to lose enthusiasm and slipped back into old, unsustainable habits. And even for those of us who persevered, there's still so much to think about – from carbon footprints and palm oil, to Fairtrade and ethical labour practices. Trying to 'make the right choice' can get really overwhelming, really quickly.

Even though my own journey into eco-friendly living overhauled my life in many ways, I still find it really difficult to be sustainable. I know that growing my own veg would be best for the planet, but my five tomato plants didn't produce a single crop last summer. I know that making my own cleaning products would be cheaper and more eco-friendly than buying them, but I never seem to find the time. I want to buy ethical fashion exclusively, but it doesn't always come in my size or budget, and I can't always find what I'm looking for second-hand. Doing extensive research into the companies I buy from is exhausting, and I can't help but feel frustrated when I see big retailers release 'conscious collections' that I know aren't as green as they seem.

Some eco swaps are easy to adopt, but once we've made the first steps it becomes harder. What happens when we can't find eco options? Once our initial rush of enthusiasm wears off, how do we turn these sustainably minded switches into long-term habits? Why is it so difficult to stop buying unsustainable products, even when we try? And are our actions even making a difference anyway? While I don't deny that most people *do* care about the planet, and more and more people are becoming aware that eco-friendly options exist in many different areas of life, I was wrong when I thought that mass adoption of these small swaps alone would be enough to change the world.

Our planet can only produce a finite number of resources, and only withstand a certain amount of heating, in order to stay healthy and continue to provide a hospitable home for human life. But in our endless pursuit of unlimited growth, we're using up natural resources quicker than nature can replenish them. We're now living in overshoot. Globally, we need 1.75 planet Earths to support humanity's current demand on the ecosystem.[2] We're also in the middle of the sixth mass extinction. Global wildlife populations have decreased by 60 per cent in our lifetime.[3] Within the next ten years, our lives will be unrecognisable if we don't take drastic action to protect the environment now.

I'm sure I don't need to tell you what eco-anxiety is, or how it's making life hard. If you've ever sat outside on a hot day, unable to fully relax in the sun because of a niggling feeling of dread, you know all too well what concern about the changing climate can do to our mental health. But unfortunately, as I'm going to show you in this book, the things you're probably doing to try to ease your eco-anxiety and have a positive impact on the planet, could in fact be making it worse. (Don't worry, I'm also going to show you what to do instead!)

The people who caused the problems are the ones now trying to sell us solutions, and the more involved in sustainable living you get, the more you begin to realise that ethical shopping alone won't solve this mess. Of course, in recent years we have witnessed brands begin to change their behaviour in response to growing consumer demand for sustainable options. But the pace of change is slow, and climate breakdown is happening too fast. Choosing the 'sustainable' option isn't always straightforward, or as effective at creating change as we would like to believe. Despite their 'conscious collections' and environmental pledges, corporations continue to pollute the planet to make a profit in pursuit of unlimited growth. Which is why the climate emergency isn't a problem we can shop our way out of.

This planet is our shared home, and we share a responsibility to leave it in a better state than we inherited it. But there are those among us who are not stepping up and doing their part. I'm not talking about your neighbour who doesn't put their recycling bin out, or your colleague who still gets their coffee in a disposable cup, because in the face of global heating, their impact, and yours, is a drop in the ocean of change we need. I'm talking about the CEOs of multinational corporations with huge carbon footprints, who mass produce the cheap stuff filling up landfills, the politicians making laws and deciding how public money is spent, the oil companies that lobby in favour of the status quo and the billionaires who have made their fortune by exploiting people and planet. They have the resources, power and influence to make big change happen fast, so they're who we need to convince. And I'm going to show you how.

For too long, corporations have shifted responsibility onto us, the consumers. Using the principle of 'Buyer Beware', whereby a buyer is responsible for what they purchase, they have made us responsible for choosing the most ethical and sustainable option, while they continue to profit regardless of which decision we make. They wield their power to influence politicians, lobby secretly against regulation and environmental action, and blame us for the state of the natural world. Now it's time for us to push back. Because our personal eco-action won't be enough unless these global power structures shift. But just because we don't have the power, money or influence of world leaders or CEOs at our finger-tips, doesn't mean we are powerless.

*

This book is for you if eco-anxiety is keeping you up at night. If you've already got your reusable coffee cup, but often find yourself wondering whether it *really* makes a difference. If you have a burning desire to tackle climate change, restore nature and fight injustice – but you haven't got the budget for high-end ethical fashion, the time, patience or desire to make your own oat milk, or the energy to research every single thing you buy, use and do. It's for you if, like me, you're tired of making sustainable sacrifices and spending hours adapting your lifestyle when nothing really seems to change, and all that recycling ends up getting burnt abroad anyway. If you're frustrated that the responsibility to make 'the right choice' always falls on your shoulders, and if you're tired of hearing politicians make empty promises in nods to the environment which ignore the true sense of urgency this crisis needs.

I want to show you how you can *really* change things. How, by working together, we can make real environmental action unavoidable for corporations. How we can create demand for sustainability in supply chains and simultaneously put pressure on political decision makers to implement legislation and systemic change that puts people and planet above profit. How we can escape manipulative marketing, buy less and be happy.

Inside this book you'll find practical tips to buy less, by avoiding the manipulative traps that advertisers use to keep us consuming, and you'll discover how this can actually make you happier, healthier and richer, despite what they want you to believe. You'll learn how to see through greenwashing, challenge the corporations who are really causing climate change and hold them accountable. And you'll discover why we all need to become climate citizens, not just consumers, and use our power as a community to build a better, more sustainable future that works for everyone, including the earth's resources. You might already be taking some of this action, or you might not have the time, energy or resources to do as much as you'd like to, and that's okay. We all need to become advocates for the type of world we want, but as you're going to see throughout this book, there are many ways to do it. I encourage you to view this as a menu of options to get you started, find what works for you, and potentially explore actions I don't talk about here too. Together we'll honestly explore what stops us from being greener, and why individual action feels insignificant in the scale of the problems our world is facing, so you're well equipped with advice and counter-arguments to share with others as you embark on your new role as an ambassador and advocate for eco-action.

*

When I was halfway through writing this book, my daughter was born slightly earlier than planned, and spent a week in the Neonatal Intensive Care Unit. On the windowsill by her incubator was a stack of books, and one night I found myself reading her what is now our favourite bedtime story – *The Snail and The Whale*. For those unfamiliar, it is a jolly tale of a snail and a whale who set out to explore the world together, revelling in its beauty and how small it makes the tiny snail feel – until one day the whale becomes beached, and it is the small but mighty snail who saves him, by uniting the community and encouraging them to take action. I love the story because it embodies the ethos behind my business, this book and the way I hope to raise my daughter – the unshakeable belief that nobody is too small to make a difference, when we work together.

Countless times in history we've seen the powerful changes that occur when ordinary people take action as a community to reshape society. Now it's our turn.

A note before we start ...

Throughout this book, you will see 'global warming' referred to as 'global heating'. This is intentional. In 2018, a scientist from the UK Met Office told the UN climate summit that this is a more accurate term in light of the risks we're facing, and the ways in which the energy balance of the planet is changing at such a rapid rate. As you'll learn in this book, the language we use is a powerful tool for inspiring action. The term 'global heating' is not used here to encourage you to feel more anxious about climate change, but instead to begin establishing a new social norm – one which is focused on taking climate action in recognition of how urgent the situation is. When something becomes the social norm, large-scale change can happen at a rapid pace, and we all have our part to play in making this happen. Changing the narrative is one way I'm playing mine.

1

Greenwashing uncovered

Pick up almost any product in the supermarket, and it's likely that you'll see some sort of eco-friendly, environmental or ethical claim on the packaging. But what does it all mean, and can you really believe the claims? Most people, when they first decide to 'be more green', start with their shopping habits. Yet even the most eco-minded consumers find all the different labels and buzzwords confusing.

A couple of years ago I found myself discussing ethical fashion with some like-minded friends. They both considered themselves to be responsible consumers, switched on to environmental issues and trying to do their bit by recycling more and making greener lifestyle choices like cycling, ditching plastic bags and eating more plant-based meals. When I asked them where they shopped for clothes, I was therefore surprised to hear them both say they were fans of the 'conscious collection' created by one of the high street's biggest fast-fashion brands. I was even more surprised when they then admitted that, although they buy these clothes, they don't actually know what the 'conscious' label means in the context of their fashion choices.

The problem is that labels like 'conscious', 'sustainable', 'biodegradable', 'natural' and to some extent even 'organic' don't come with enough regulation around their usage to ensure that brands have the credentials to back up these claims. There are no industry standard definitions in place, leaving these popular terms open to interpretation (and manipulation) by advertisers. In the case of my friends' favourite 'conscious collection', the retailer uses the term 'conscious' to refer to the percentage of organic materials and recycled fabrics in the clothes – *not* the overall sustainability of the company or ethical practices in the supply chain.

In fact, a few months after our conversation, this particular retailer was criticised by the Norwegian Consumer Authority (CA) for misleading marketing of its 'sustainable' collection, with the CA's director stating that the information given about their sustainability practices was insufficient and 'did not specify the actual environmental benefit' – warning consumers that they may be being misled by statements in the company's marketing strategies.

The CA concluded that the brand's portrayal of their sustainability was in breach of Norwegian marketing laws, and was being used 'to deceive consumers on the nature of a product, causing them to make an economic decision that they would not otherwise have made'.

CA director Elisabeth Lier Haugseth encouraged companies to be more specific when advertising sustainability, saying: 'The focus should be on what your company is actually doing to be more sustainable, and refrain from using general terms such as "sustainable", "environmentally friendly" and "green".'[1]

Fashion brands can use all the recycled materials and innovative plant-based fibres they like, but until they stop churning out a new collection every week, selling clothes cheaply, exploiting their workforce and suppliers to keep costs low and margins high, and encouraging us to consume clothes as if they were disposable, they can never truly be sustainable. Yet with so much eco-friendly product labelling, it was no wonder my friends were confused. This problem isn't exclusive to the fashion industry. Confusing labelling is everywhere.

Did you know that the 'Green Dot' symbol (the arrow in a circle which usually appears in black and white on labels) doesn't mean the packaging is recyclable, will be recycled or has been recycled, despite what many people think? It's actually a trademark used on packaging in some European countries, which signifies that the producer has made a financial contribution towards the recovery and recycling of packaging in Europe. Companies pay a fee to be able to use the logo, and the fees are cheaper if they make the packaging recyclable, but it's not a requirement.

With so many different buzzwords for sustainability, confusing symbols and inconsistencies in marketing messaging, it's no surprise that we struggle to know what's eco-friendly, even when we try to shop consciously. Unfortunately, in many cases, this confusion is no accident.

Many companies actually invest more money into looking ethical and sustainable in their marketing efforts than in changing their materials, supply chains and business practices – a rising trend known as 'greenwashing'.

While some greenwashing is unintentional, resulting from a lack of sustainability knowledge or complete supply chain consideration, the majority of cases are, sadly, completely intentional – designed to cash in on growing consumer demand for sustainability in a way that maximises shareholder profit. This dangerous trend not only misleads well-meaning consumers, it also diverts valuable attention from true sustainability initiatives and creates a corporate culture with a dangerous lack of accountability when it comes to environmental action.

The seven sins of greenwashing

In 2007, TerraChoice, an environmental marketing firm later acquired by UL, developed The Seven Sins of Greenwashing in an attempt to help consumers identify products making misleading environmental claims.

In a 2008–9 study, they found that more than 98 per cent of 'green' products in stores across the US, Canada, Australia and the UK were guilty of at least one of these sins:

1. The hidden trade-off

Labelling a product as environmentally friendly based on a narrow set of emphasised attributes, when other attributes not addressed might have a bigger impact on the eco-friendliness of the product as a whole

Charity T-shirts often inadvertently undermine the environmental causes they set out to support. Many 'save the bees' slogan T-shirts are not made from organic cotton, which means that the cotton used has been grown with pesticides and fertilisers – harmful chemicals that are killing the bees and pollinators which the T-shirts set out to raise funds for in the first place.

Similarly, many 'save the ocean' T-shirts are made from synthetic materials which shed micro-plastics when they're washed.

These tiny plastic particles find their way into our waterways, ending up in the ocean where they cause plastic pollution and harm to marine life.[2]

While greenwashing focuses on environmental and sustainability claims, many brands have also been accused of 'purpose washing', as rising interest in social justice has led conscious consumers to consider the ethical credentials of the products they purchase too.

A purpose washing scandal hit the charity sector when girl band the Spice Girls teamed up with Comic Relief in 2019, to release a charity T-shirt bearing the message '#IWannaBeASpiceGirl', as part of the charity's gender justice campaign. Money raised from sales of the T-shirts was donated to Comic Relief's fund to help 'champion equality for women', with the charity receiving £11.60 from the retail price of £19.40 per T-shirt. However, it was later revealed that the T-shirts were being made by workers in Bangladesh who were earning significantly less than a living wage. Reports suggested that women were paid the equivalent of 35p an hour and facing verbal abuse and harassment inside the factory producing the 'feminist' T-shirts.[3]

2. No proof

Environmental claims are not backed up by accessible supporting information, factual evidence or third-party certification

Fast-food chain Burger King came under fire in 2020 for greenwashed claims about 'reduced methane beef'. They ran a video commercial announcing that going forward they would be using meat from cows that they claimed released 33 per cent less methane – achieved by introducing lemongrass into their diet to improve digestion.

Beef farming is extremely greenhouse-gas intensive. It's

estimated that 3.5 per cent of all greenhouse gas emissions since 1990 have been methane from cows and sheep – and if cows and sheep had their own country, it would be the fifth largest greenhouse-gas emitter in the world! Burger King claimed that their new lemongrass feed leads to a 33 per cent methane reduction, but they released a summary of their research and the commercial before the results had been peer reviewed, meaning that they had no proof that the results were scientifically valid.[4] There's no reason to believe that the science is false, but it's bad practice to publicly broadcast results, and use them in advertising to highlight environmental credentials, without external verification.

Digging into the write-up, it is revealed that the lemongrass diet is only given to cows during the last three to four months of their life. Beef cows typically live around eighteen months before they are slaughtered, which would suggest that they are only fed the methane-reducing lemongrass diet for less than a quarter of their life.

Methane emissions aren't, however, the only environmental concern when it comes to animal agriculture. Cattle farming is one of the leading causes of deforestation in the Amazon rainforest, and when trees are cut down stored carbon is released and the rainforest's ability to remove carbon dioxide from the atmosphere is lowered. Even if the greenhouse gas savings from the lemongrass beef were 33 per cent, the environmental impact of a beef burger would still be six times higher than its plant-based alternative!

3. Vagueness
Using terms that are too broad or poorly defined, so that the meaning is likely to be misunderstood by the consumer

The term 'natural' is a prime example of this – arsenic and mercury are naturally occurring, and highly poisonous! 'Natural' skincare products often draw a higher price point and attract eco-conscious consumers, but you wouldn't want to see these on the ingredients list!

In 2016 UK supermarket Tesco were accused of trying to mislead customers by using British-sounding farm names on their 'value range' fresh food products. It was revealed that many of the farms were fake, and those that did exist were not supplying the retailer. The campaign group Feedback called the supermarket out for 'deliberately encouraging consumers to believe that the meat is sourced from small-scale producers'.[5]

Despite their deliberate choice of British-sounding farm names – designed to evoke images of idyllic, small-scale farms in the British countryside (and drawing on consumers' assumptions about what that means for the quality of the produce), the supermarket's website acknowledged that these ranges don't necessarily come from the UK. But this relies on the time-poor consumer to do their research; to look beyond the label and uncover the truth. Even if we did have time to do this for every product we buy, if we trust the brand we're buying from, we're unlikely to question it anyway. Which is what Tesco were relying on when they used the power of vague branding instead of robust sourcing to boost sales of their value range.

4. Worshipping false labels

Implying that a product has third-party endorsement or certification to make consumers believe that it went through a legitimate screening process, when no such endorsement exists

One prolific example of this is companies using a rabbit symbol on their packaging to show that they are 'against animal testing'.

Animal testing policies are often filled with loopholes. No brand wants to admit that their products or ingredients have harmed animals, and thanks to a lack of regulation in this area, they don't have to. The burden of proof currently falls to brands that truly are cruelty-free, and there are limited ways to prove it because the term 'cruelty-free' is not regulated or monitored.

Brands may say they are cruelty-free, but actually outsource animal testing in their supply chain. This excuse is commonly used by companies importing and selling their products in mainland China, where animal testing was, until recently, required by law. (The laws in China did change in 2021, lifting the requirement for some imported cosmetics, if they have the proper certificates and documentation required. This means that brands will have to jump through hoops to avoid animal testing and might still test as an easier route to market.) Many cosmetics companies will use wording to state that their products aren't tested on animals, but cover up the fact that the ingredients in the products were. There is also an issue around raw material suppliers using animal tests, which companies don't have to disclose.

Unfortunately, the Advertising Standards Agency in the UK considers 'cruelty-free' to be evaluated at a product level, rather than a brand level. The responsibility to research a brand's credentials and track record remains with the consumer as they evaluate their purchasing decision.

Products will often come with a bunny icon on the packaging to symbolise their stance against animal testing, but they can't always be trusted. Unless they are an official trademark from an established, reputable, third-party organisation (like the official Leaping Bunny accreditation), makeshift bunny logos and icons are meaningless, and simply designed to mislead time-poor consumers.

In order for a company or product to be certified as cruelty-free, they must meet a set of independently verified criteria and demonstrate proof to a third party. This often also involves paying a licensing fee to carry the official cruelty-free logo from that organisation (which can be a barrier for small brands, but they still shouldn't use their own unofficial versions).

Always look for labels and logos which are certified by third-party organisations. For cruelty-free products, these include:

The Leaping Bunny

Cruelty Free International also have an online database of beauty brands that are Leaping Bunny approved. You can search this at: https://www.crueltyfreeinternational.org/LeapingBunny

PETA's Beauty Without Bunnies logos

Worshipping false labels is not a problem reserved only for the cosmetics industry.

One of the most well-known labels in conscious consumerism is the Fairtrade mark. A globally recognised symbol, it demonstrates a product's commitment to ethical trading with high social, labour and environmental standards, with third-party verification that consumers can trust. Yet some retailers are choosing to use their own schemes, with no official accreditation or logo, instead.

Disappointingly, in 2017, Sainsbury's supermarket, the world's largest retailer of Fairtrade products, announced plans to drop the official Fairtrade mark from their own-brand teas and replace it with an in-house certification scheme, using the phrase 'fairly traded' instead.[6] A year earlier, the UK's best-known chocolate brand, Cadbury, ended its affiliation with Fairtrade, as parent company Mondelez moved to bring all Cadbury lines under its in-house environmental and labour policy scheme, Coca Life.

In-house schemes potentially provide more flexibility, as well as cost savings, allowing brands to meet commitments across a range of social and environmental priorities. But without third-party audit and verifications, brands are left to mark their own homework, and there's no guarantee that they're living up to the commitments they've made. The responsibility falls to the consumer to research each individual scheme and the standards they claim to uphold – without one easily recognisable, trusted brand to look out for.

5. Irrelevance

Making an environmental claim that may be true, but is unimportant or unhelpful and may be intentionally misleading

Baby bottles sold in the USA might claim to be free from BPA – a chemical which scientists fear may cause breast cancer, heart disease, obesity and other conditions. However, this would be irrelevant because the Food and Drug Administration (FDA) have banned the use of BPA in these products in America. Therefore, by default all baby bottles in the USA are BPA free, so trying to highlight this as a selling point could be seen as misleading. But irrelevance isn't always this obvious and easy to spot.

In 2018, following a shocking viral video of a sea turtle having a plastic straw painfully extracted from its nose, as part of a growing wave of public awareness of plastic pollution, calls to ban single-use plastic straws were getting louder, and brands were keen to show their support.

Starbucks announced that they would eliminate single-use plastic straws from their stores worldwide by 2020, making alternative-material straws available for those who need them, but replacing the plastic straws with new, sippable strawless lids. They estimated that the move would eliminate more than 1 billion straws a year. But they were quickly criticised, and their claims became irrelevant, when it was revealed that the strawless lids (which were still single-use) would require more plastic than the current lids and plastic straws combined.

Starbucks defended the decision by stating that the strawless lid would be more commonly accepted in recycling schemes, and that straws are often too small and lightweight to be captured by recycling equipment. However, environmental campaigners were quick to point out that only 9 per cent of the world's plastic is recycled, and yet again this leaves responsibility with the consumer to 'do the right thing' when disposing of the product, even when the infrastructure to do so may not be easily accessible or convenient.

They weren't the only brand to come under fire for their greenwashed approach to the single-use plastic problem. McDonald's replaced plastic straws with paper alternatives, but these couldn't be recycled at all, due to lack of infrastructure in the UK.

The two companies later announced plans to work together on a global recyclable and/or compostable cup solution, but the move was met with scepticism as Starbucks had previously pledged a decade earlier to make 100 per cent of its cups reusable or recyclable by 2015, which still hasn't happened.[7]

6. Lesser of two evils

Claiming to be more environmentally friendly than other products in the same category, when the category as a whole is known to be environmentally unfriendly

'Organic' cigarettes may sound greener, but they're still toxic!

In 2008, budget airline EasyJet ran an advert in the UK national press claiming that its plane emitted 22 per cent less carbon dioxide than other planes on the same route. But the advert didn't make it clear that the figure related to emissions *per passenger*, and the airline was able to reduce emissions per passenger simply because the plane could carry more people than traditional airlines. The brand was reprimanded by the Advertising Standards Agency, which said:

> We concluded that, because the basis for the claim had not been fully explained, the ad misleadingly implied that EasyJet planes were more environmentally efficient than the aircraft used by traditional airlines.[8]

7. Fibbing

Advertising environmental claims which are simply false

Dubbed the 'diesel dupe', the Volkswagen emissions scandal is perhaps the most prolific example of greenwashing lies.

In 2015, the Environmental Protection Agency (EPA) found that many VW cars being sold in America were cheating emissions tests. Software in the engine could detect when it was being tested, changing performance levels accordingly to improve results.[9]

VW had undertaken a huge marketing push in the US, highlighting the cars' low emissions, but in truth, their engines were emitting up to 40 times more than the permitted levels of nitrogen oxide pollutants. The EPA uncovered 482,000 affected cars in America, but VW admitted that around 11 million cars worldwide were fitted with the 'defeat device' responsible for the false results.

Millions of cars worldwide were recalled, and the company set aside $18 billion to cover costs and fines associated with the scandal, which left them reporting their first quarterly loss for fifteen years and facing fines from the EPA.

Looking beyond the labels

From food to fashion, cosmetics to cars, and almost every industry in between, greenwashing and purpose washing are rife, as brands try to capture the growing attention of the ethical and eco market.

In their study, TerraChoice found 'no proof' and 'vagueness' to be the most commonly committed greenwashing sins. Often these two will be used together to mislead consumers, and it's not uncommon to find brands and products guilty of more than one of these sins.

Of course, there are other, less obvious types of greenwashing too. Many advertisers will use images of leaves, animals and nature, or minimalist packaging design to imply a more 'natural' edge to the brand. Others will be less subtle and will literally make their packaging green in colour.

Some may not intend to greenwash, but will fail to consider the impact of their whole supply chain, or simply lack the knowledge to embed sustainability properly. Others know exactly what they're doing. In 2000, oil company British Petroleum hired an advertising firm to launch a $200 million rebranding campaign, which saw them rename as BP and adopt the slogan 'Beyond Petroleum'. The logo got a new look with a green, yellow and white sunburst and gas stations were redecorated with 'green' imagery.

But the company failed to live up to their new green identity. In March 2006, a BP oil pipeline caused one of Alaska's biggest ever oil spills, and in 2010 the Deepwater Horizon oil rig exploded, causing the largest marine oil spill in history.[10]

A visual rebrand and carefully constructed marketing strategy isn't enough to attract eco-minded consumers, or to protect the planet. And you only have to look at the amount of rainbow branding used on products and adverts during Pride celebrations to see how many advertisers are trying to 'purpose wash' their way into more conscious markets using social causes now too.

Environmental and social movements are being commodified by marketers, but at what cost? All these labels and claims are confusing for the time-poor consumer, and the pressure is yet again on us to do our research before we buy and 'make the right choice' – which means that change isn't happening at the scale and pace we need.

So, what can we do?

Learn to spot greenwashing

Unfortunately, while it remains unregulated, the responsibility falls to us, the consumers, to challenge and avoid greenwashing when we shop, which is easier said than done. The more demand there is for ethical and sustainable products, the more advertisers will invest in greenwashing campaigns – and their methods to deceive us are getting smarter.

Often, it's hard to detect when we're being greenwashed because advertising is designed to appeal to us subconsciously. Marketers don't want us thinking too much about our purchases, or we might question whether we really need them and decide not to buy. We really do need to be 'conscious' consumers when we're looking at buying anything and make sure we do our research first.

The best starting point is to learn the Seven Sins of Greenwashing. You could even keep a list in your wallet to remind yourself what to look out for while you shop.

Planning ahead is also important. You're more likely to get greenwashed when you're making impulse decisions or rushing to find something in the supermarket. By planning ahead, you can make sure you're only buying what you need (the most sustainable choice you can make is to buy less), and do your research into a product and brand's sustainable credentials and the track record of the business behind it before you buy.

And remember, not all greenwashing falls neatly into the Seven Sins. If you feel that a product, its packaging or advertising is giving you the impression that it is good for the environment, the best thing you can do is question it further.

Prioritise

There's no such thing as 100 per cent ethical or sustainable, so any brands that make grand claims about their environmental credentials should be approached with caution. However, this also means that as consumers, we can't expect the products we buy to be perfect until the entire system changes.

The best place to start is to identify which issues are most important to you and prioritise these when you shop. Trying to make the most ethical and sustainable choice involves a lot of research, and you'll often find yourself having to compromise in one area to be as eco as possible in another.

Do you want to tackle plastic pollution in the ocean by reducing the amount of single use plastic you consume? Are you concerned about deforestation in the rainforest? If so, you may want to choose products that only use sustainable palm oil – or boycott it altogether. Is it important to you that no harmful chemicals are used to produce the products you buy? If you're keen to go natural and protect pollinators, then choosing organic might be your top priority.

Of course, in an ideal world we'd be able to achieve all of these things easily, but sadly too many products on the market today come with ethical dilemmas and compromises must be made. We've all come across Fairtrade bananas wrapped in plastic, unlike their less ethical counterparts. Decide what you're willing to compromise on, and what values and standards are non-negotiable for you, and let these be your guide when you buy.

Don't be afraid to ask

Once you've narrowed down your priorities, you'll find it easier to research the products you purchase regularly and make yourself a 'safe list' of brands. This will take time, so don't put pressure on yourself to do it all at once. It can be helpful to go room by room through your house, product by product, gradually doing the research and swapping to more sustainable options.

In the past, you had to write letters to brands to find information about their ethical and sustainable credentials, and you might have found yourself easily ignored. Thankfully, today, almost every business has an online presence. When we question brands publicly on social media, they feel greater pressure to respond, and if their answers aren't up to scratch, we can push for more evidence and call out greenwashing, which can lead to change.

It takes time to research the ethical and sustainable credentials of a brand, and it would be impossible to do it for every single product that we buy. But big companies employ people to run their social media for them, and it's their job to know the answers to these questions – or to find out if they don't have that information to hand. They get paid to do the work, you don't. Asking a quick question on Twitter, Instagram, Facebook or another platform where you're already active and interacting with brands only takes a couple of minutes out of your day, but it holds them accountable to providing the answers – and the more they get asked, the more they realise that consumer pressure is growing and can't be escaped, which will help incentivise them to clean up their act.

If you suspect greenwashing, or you're forced to make a compromise on values that matter to you, tell the brand. Transparency is the first step to more ethical and sustainable business. If corporations are open and honest about what they're doing, and where the limitations are, we can start to have the productive conversations that lead to new innovations and improvements. But if they continue to cover up their bad behaviour and get away with it, nothing will change.

Genuinely ethical and sustainable brands won't be afraid to answer tough questions. They'll have evidence to back up their claims, and they'll be willing to discuss their limitations and roadmap for improvement too. However, if you get sent links to their sustainability pages on their website, remember to look for the greenwashing warning signs – especially vagueness, no proof and false labels. Don't be afraid to ask for clarity.

My husband almost learnt this the hard way. As parents-to-be, we were busy stocking up on all the essential supplies a new baby needs, and one afternoon as he was scrolling through Instagram, an advert for 'biodegradable and compostable baby wipes' caught his attention. The company claimed to make it easy for new parents to go green, by offering a subscription of their '100% plastic free' plant-based wipes. A compelling video showed a scientist talking about how the wipes would break down in compost, giving her endorsement to a product she had been initially sceptical about.

He told me he was signing us up, but first I needed to see their credentials:

'What are they made from?'

'How quickly do they degrade?'

'Have they been tested in landfill?'

'Can they go in the home compost bin, or do they need to go into industrial compost, because we don't have that around here?'

As I began to fire questions at him, I could see him looking more and more confused, and understandably so. A quick look at the website and I saw that, on the surface, the company were saying all the right things.

They're a small business 'taking on the big guys'. Unlike their competitors, their wipes were '100% plastic free'. Their packaging was '100% recyclable' – although from the photo the wipes appeared to still come in a plastic wrap, which immediately made me question their '100% plastic-free' claim. And they proudly displayed badges from the British Skin Foundation, showing that their products were suitable for eczema, allergy friendly, Made in Britain and vegan. All credentials which are important to new parents, and likely to appeal to conscious consumers, but which don't clarify the sustainability of the materials they're using. It was either a genuine commitment to being as ethical and sustainable as possible, or an attempt to distract and misguide consumers, similar to techniques used in the 'hidden trade off' sin.

As consumers have become more concerned about their plastic footprint in recent years, 'biodegradable' and 'compostable' alternatives have become increasingly popular. But these are unregulated terms, and much like the confusing 'conscious fashion collection', many consumers don't actually know what they mean – they just assume they're good for the planet.

Although these labels often appear on packaging together, the two aren't interchangeable. 'Biodegradable' means that the material is capable of being decomposed, so it will break down and return to nature. 'Compostable' materials are made of organic matter and also break down, but they go one step further and actually make nutrient-rich compost as they decay.

However, because the terms are unregulated, 'biodegradable' products or packaging don't have to declare how long they take to break down, or what conditions they need to do so. Even plastic (which will be around for thousands of years) could technically be labelled as biodegradable, because it will break down eventually. But when it does, it doesn't 'return to the earth', it just becomes smaller and smaller pieces of plastic. These harmful microplastics are polluting the planet and even finding their way into our bodies by entering the food chain – and we don't know what long-term impact this is having on our health.

Plus, biodegradable plastics can't be recycled, because they contain extra chemicals (and actually take more resources to create than normal plastics), so when they are thrown away, they end up in landfill. Landfill conditions are not optimal – they usually lack the heat, light and oxygen needed for biodegradable materials to break down, so just because something is capable of it, doesn't mean that it actually does when it ends up on the trash heap.

That's why it's so important to ask any manufacturer claiming that their products or packaging are biodegradable whether they've been landfill tested, and what the exact timeline for breakdown is. If they can't provide clear answers, it's likely that they haven't tested them and may not be as eco-friendly as they claim.

The same applies to 'compostable' labels too. Not all compostable products will break down properly in home compost systems – some require the sustained temperatures of industrial composting systems, which aren't available in many residential areas. Commercial composting centres also have machinery such as chippers and mixers which can help to ensure that all items reach more ideal composting conditions, to accelerate and aid the process. They can monitor and control moisture and airflow to make sure there are no harmful bacteria being cultivated, in ways that we can't achieve at home, and although the soil produced at the end is the same, there are elements of the process which mean some compostable products are only suitable for industrial composting. But manufacturers don't have to clarify this on their labelling. And just like biodegradable options, if they haven't been landfill tested, there's no guarantee that these compostable options will be better for the environment if they're not disposed of correctly.

I took to Twitter to ask the baby wipe brand for more clarity about whether their '100% biodegradable and compostable' wipes were suitable for home compost, if they had been tested in landfill and what the timeline for their breakdown was.

The initial response I got was that the wipes could go in the home compost, but they recommend disposing of them in general waste (destined for landfill) 'where they will go on to naturally biodegrade'. I had to go back to them for further clarity about how long this would take. Their follow-up response focused on their natural ingredients (not what I'd asked them about – irrelevance). They reassured me that they '*should*' degrade in landfill where conditions are designed for anaerobic degradation (no evidence provided to support this vague claim) and directed me to a video showing the composting process compared to that of a competitor product. Although their wipes had broken down in the home compost, there was still no clarity around the timeline for this – the video just cut to 'a few months later …', again relying on vagueness.

Baby wipes and other disposables are highly problematic for the environment, and at the moment these 'biodegradables' probably are the best solution on the market. On one hand, they are entitled to market themselves as a leader, proudly showcase the improvements they've made to be more environmentally friendly, and use their platform to educate consumers about why competitor products are bad for the planet. But on the other hand, elements of their messaging border on greenwashing. By celebrating their progress without discussing the limitations, or how far the industry still needs to go, they may falsely give the impression that no more work needs to be done. Ultimately, this approach will only leave us with 'better' products to choose from which sadly still aren't as good for the environment as we are led to believe.

Know the right questions to ask

Part of the reason that lots of greenwashing goes unchallenged is because consumers don't know what questions to ask. We may recognise that we can't always take eco labels at face value, but we don't always know how to challenge them effectively. This varies from issue to issue, and will largely be product-dependent, but once you've identified your own sustainability priorities, you can begin to learn about the key concerns involved without getting overwhelmed.

Take my fashion-consuming friends for example. If they had stopped to consider what they want from their clothes, they might have dug a little deeper into the 'conscious' label they were buying. If organic materials or reducing plastic were priorities for them, they might feel comfortable buying from this fast-fashion brand, because the 'conscious collection' refers to the percentage of recycled plastic used to make polyester fabric, or the percentage of organic cotton in the garments. But if tackling waste was their main concern, they may decide to avoid a fast-fashion retailer, where the business model is based on churning out up to 52 micro-collections of new clothes a year, and opt to shop second-hand for clothes already in circulation instead.

When I first decided to switch the contents of my make-up bag to cruelty-free options only, I didn't realise that animal testing was a legal requirement in China. I took brands at face value when their packaging carried a random bunny logo, or their website proudly proclaimed that they were cruelty-free, until I dug deeper into the issue and learnt about this legal loophole from a beauty blogger. I then had to go back to the brands I was buying from and ask them more questions about what markets they sell in, and whether they outsource animal testing to external suppliers.

I also had to make a personal decision about whether to buy cruelty-free lines from brands that make other products, or choose to support a completely cruelty-free business. On one hand, buying a cruelty-free range from a bigger brand or parent company sends them a signal about consumer demand for cruelty-free products. Many conscious consumers will argue that this encourages brands to invest in their ethical and sustainable lines – and data would suggest that this is true. In 2018, Unilever's 28 Sustainable Living brands grew 69 per cent faster than the rest of the business,[11] and in 2019 the company announced plans to sell off all brands that do not contribute positively to society.[12]

But at the same time, if you buy a sustainable range or from a subsidiary company, the profits all ultimately go to the same place, so buying from a bigger brand is still supporting shareholders who don't share your values. Again, this is a personal decision each conscious consumer needs to make, and it begins with asking some tough questions.

Four questions every company should be able to answer

The most important sustainability question to ask when you're shopping is: 'Do I really need this?' To be more sustainable, we all need to consume less. Start by asking yourself if you really need what you're about to buy, and if so, can you borrow it or get it second-hand?

If you do need to buy new, then you'll want to try to avoid greenwashing and spend your money with a company that is truly committed to sustainability. The research you'll need to do will depend on what type of product you're looking for, but to get you started, here are four questions that every company should be able to answer about their sustainability:

1. ***Are you actively working to reduce your carbon footprint?***
   Conscious collections and eco ranges are often considered greenwashing when the company isn't doing anything else to reduce their carbon footprint or environmental impact. The company should ideally be monitoring their environmental impact, setting clear targets to reduce it and transparently reporting their

progress. Beware any companies that claim to be 100 per cent sustainable, or make bold statements without evidence. Watch out for carbon offsetting promises too – it's important to reduce emissions, not just offset them. Sustainable companies should be able to tell you how they're reducing their reliance on fossil fuels and moving towards renewables.

2. *Are you producing at a sustainable rate?*
Many industries are over-producers, encouraging mass consumption at cheap prices to maximise profit margins. This means more extraction, emissions and waste. Pay attention to how often brands have new product releases and how often they're on sale or clearance – these should be red flags that they're encouraging mass consumption.

3. *Can you provide evidence for your environmental claims?*
Brands should be able to explain what sustainability means to them, and any environmental claims made should be 'clear, based on well-accepted science, justifiable, qualified with evidence and based on a full lifecycle assessment (unless otherwise stated)', according to the UK's Advertising Standards Agency.[13]

4. *How do you take responsibility for reducing waste and managing your products at the end of their life?*
When it comes to waste reduction, most companies are focusing on their packaging – which is important, but it's only one part of their waste footprint. Currently, the responsibility for disposing of things usually falls to the end user, so it's important we do our research. Is the product easy to repair to prolong its life? Will the company help? Is it recyclable, and if not, will it break down in landfill in a reasonable amount of time?

Would his teaching position be so important to him that he'd kill to keep it?

My phone buzzes to life in my pocket, interrupting my thoughts. I answer the phone absentmindedly.

"Hey, Vee. What's up?" Rollins's voice sounds strained.

"Listen, I'm kind of busy. What do you need?" I wince as soon as the words are out of my mouth. They sound terrible.

"Look. I'm trying to make an effort."

I take a deep breath. "I know. I'm sorry. Things are just really stressful. An officer was here, questioning my sister."

"Really?"

"Yeah. It was messed up."

We're both quiet for a second.

"Hey, I'm sorry I haven't been around much lately," he says. "I'm kind of going through some intense stuff of my own."

I think of how he's never let me visit his house. What's going on over there?

"You want to talk about it?"

"No. It's personal." His voice sounds strangled, like he wants to tell me what's going on with him but can't bring himself to spill his guts. I know how that feels. I wish, more than anything, that he felt comfortable sharing his problems, but how can I pressure him when I have my own secrets?

"Well. If you ever want to talk, you know I'm here."

"I know," he says. "Hey. We cool?"

"We cool," I reply. "Wanna go to a funeral with me tomorrow?"

CHAPTER TWELVE

Mattie rides silently in the back of Rollins's car. We circle the parking lot, looking for an available space, but there's nothing. Even the handicapped spots are all full. We have to park on the street a block down from the funeral home and walk the rest of the way.

Wind sweeps through my hair and chills my skin. Normally I wouldn't think twice about huddling next to Rollins for warmth, but our relationship seems fragile now, like a bone that's broken and not yet fully healed. It seems safer to keep to myself.

We are a parade of black. Rollins wears jeans, a black button-down shirt, and a skinny black tie. I picked out a pair of simple black pants and a nice black shirt edged with dark-purple lace. My sister is wearing the slinky black dress she'd planned on wearing to homecoming. I didn't have the heart to point out how inappropriate it was. She doesn't really own any other black clothes.

Despite the chill in the air outside, it feels like an oven when we push into the building. The place is packed wall to wall with people, who drift from one homemade Sophie photo collage to another, as if they're in a museum.

In one picture, Sophie looks about age six, chubby in a blue tutu and mouse nose and whiskers and ears. In another, she hooks her arms around Mattie's and Amber's shoulders, all of them in their cheerleading uniforms. Time spins backward in another picture, and baby Sophie plays in a duck-shaped bathtub, a washcloth modestly placed over her girly parts.

Sophie's mother bustles over, her teased hair leading the way, and gives Mattie a hug. Tears squeeze out of her eyes, blue makeup running in streams through the creases in her face. She looks haggard.

"I'm so glad you could make it," she says, and Mattie reaches her arms around Mrs. Jacobs for a hug.

"I'm sorry," Mattie whispers. The words are not enough, can never be enough, and it's like we're all standing around the growing hole of how *not enough* they are. Sophie's mom squeezes Mattie once more and leaves to make her rounds.

We trudge toward the next room, where rows upon rows of folding chairs have been set up. Most of them are already taken by Sophie's extended family and teachers and what seems like every kid in the whole school. We're lucky to find three seats in the back.

I sit between Mattie and Rollins and crane my head, searching every face, but I don't see anyone I'm looking for. No Amber. No Scotch. No Mr. Golden.

It takes about fifteen minutes for everyone to get settled. Tons of people have to stand in the back of the sweltering room. They fan themselves with programs that have Sophie's school picture on the front cover.

The coffin is at the front, flanked by long white candles and great bouquets of lilies. Thank god it's a closed casket. I don't know if I could take seeing her again. My sister sobs quietly next to me. I take her hand.

A slim man in a blue suit finds his way to the front and stands before the casket, his hands hovering just above the white wood, but not touching it. He stands there reverently for a moment, and everyone tries not to stare. Someone behind me whispers that he's Sophie's father. He turns around to face us, his lower lip wobbling, but he composes himself long enough to read a poem he has written.

Almost everyone's head is down, giving the man his time to mourn, but I'm looking around the room, hoping to spot one of my suspects, to see how they're reacting to all this.

After the man has finished his poem, an old woman plays a piano in the corner. I mutter something about having to go to the bathroom and manage to edge my way out of our row and through the crowd without sticking my butt in anyone's face or knocking anyone over.

I duck out a door in the back that leads to a smaller room with a blue couch and an end table loaded with boxes of Kleenex. There's a pop machine and a water cooler in the corner. Doors on either side of the room lead to the bathrooms. I go to the door marked Ladies and put my ear to the door. I hear a strange sound coming from the ladies' room—almost like honking.

I twist the knob and push open the door just a crack, enough to peek inside and see who's making the terrible noise. Crumpled on the floor with a wad of toilet paper woven around her fingers, Amber Prescott is falling apart.

I slip into the room and close the door behind me. Then I sink to the floor and sit across from Amber, cross-legged. I don't say anything, don't even look at her. I just sit and breathe. And wait.

Amber stops crying long enough to recognize who's in the room with her, but then she continues on, louder than ever. In her place, I would have shouted to get the hell out. I don't do anything but let her raw emotion wash over me. Though it seems like she's truly devastated, I can't help but wonder how much of what I'm seeing is guilt. Guilt for destroying her best friend.

Just when I start to think about going to get her a cup of water, she stops crying. She uses the toilet paper to clean up the mascara that's run all over her face. I stand up and turn on the water for her, then step out of the way so she can wash her face.

She doesn't say anything to me, just gives me this kind of grateful look before she unlocks the door and slinks out. When she leaves, I glance in the mirror, at the girl with the pink pigtails tied with black ribbons, and all I feel is shame. Amber may have ruined Sophie, but I stood by and let her. I knew Amber and Mattie were planning something horrible, and I didn't do one damn thing to stop them.

As I open the door to leave, I notice something silver shining on the floor. I stoop down and realize it's a tiny diamond earring—the kind that Amber always wears. I scoop it up and hurry out of the bathroom to see if I can catch her, but I don't see her anywhere. I tuck the earring into my pocket.

The funeral has ended, and people have formed small clusters around the lobby.

I spot Mattie in a huddle of cheerleaders doing some sort of group hug, but I don't see Rollins anywhere, so I go outside. Just as I'd guessed, Rollins is standing several yards away from the funeral home, a cigarette tucked discreetly behind his back.

"Everyone's saying Sophie was pregnant," Rollins says, taking a quick drag and then hiding the cigarette again.

I sigh. "Yeah. The officer mentioned something about it yesterday."

"You have any idea who the father could be?" Rollins releases a puff of smoke.

"I have a few theories," I reply. "The front-runner is Scotch Becker."

Rollins drops the cigarette and grinds it into the cement with the heel of his boot. "Scum."

"Pretty much."

A hand on my back makes me jump. Turning, I see Mattie's teary face.

"You ready to go?" I ask. Earlier, Mattie had cried that she didn't want to go to the burial. She didn't want to see Sophie's casket lowered into the ground. I can't say I blame her.

"Actually," she says, "I think I'm going to stay. Sam can

give me a ride." She glances behind her, and I follow her gaze to Samantha Phillips, who stands twirling her keys. When she sees me looking, her face goes slack and she turns to face the other way.

"Are you sure?" I ask.

She nods.

"Okay, I'll see you at home."

I watch her return to the group of cheerleaders. It seems strange—of all the people saying goodbye to Sophie today, I'm the only one who knows how she truly left this world. The knowledge settles at the bottom of my stomach and weighs me down like cement.

Rollins squeezes my shoulder. "Let's go."

CHAPTER THIRTEEN

Long after Rollins drops me off, I sit on the swing on our front porch. I don't want to go inside. The house is so empty. So silent. I don't want to be alone with my memory of Sophie's death. I don't want to risk falling asleep and having to face her accusations again. Outside, the wind keeps me awake. That, and the caffeine pills.

I shake some more into my hand, pop them into my mouth, and crunch them into powder.

A breeze blows through the large oak tree, coaxing even more leaves to fall. Down the street, a movement catches my eye. A tall boy with a cobalt sweatshirt and blond hair is making his way toward me on a skateboard. As he gets closer, I see that it's Zane Huxley. And he's looking in my direction. My stomach does a little somersault.

He coasts to a stop in front of my house, flips up his skateboard, and takes a few steps toward the porch. "Hey," he says, an unmistakable look of pleasure crossing his face.

I nod at him, swallowing the caffeine powder so I can speak. "Hey. Enjoying your afternoon off from school?"

"Yeah. Did you go to the funeral?"

"Yeah. It was . . . unfathomable," I say, unable to find a more fitting word for the funeral of a teenager. "What are you doing here, anyway?"

I feel dumb and want to take back the question. It sounds like I don't want him here, when I do. I want someone to talk to. Someone who didn't know Sophie, someone who doesn't know about me and my narcolepsy and how messed up everything is.

Luckily, he just laughs. "Good to see you, too. We live over on Arbor Lane, at the end of the street."

"The blue one with the picket fence? That's been for sale forever."

An awkward silence passes between us. I try to think of something funny or clever or *anything* to say. I don't want to be alone with my thoughts anymore.

Another gust of wind rips through the yard, sending a chill through me. I shiver.

"Hey, do you want to come in? I could make some coffee or something."

"Sure. Little chilly outside."

I get up and open the door, and he props up his skateboard outside and follows me into the house. In the kitchen, he pulls out a stool and sits with his elbows on the counter. I whisk two coffee mugs—one from the University of Iowa and one that says "Bestest Dad in the World"—out of the cupboard and set them between us. He's quiet as I make the coffee, and it reminds me of sitting in the bathroom of the funeral home, giving Amber the time to put herself back together.

I fill each mug with steaming black liquid. In the refrigerator, I find half a gallon of skimmed milk. I dump some in my cup and then spoon in some sugar. After stirring it for a few seconds, I take a sip.

Over the rim of my cup, I watch Zane stirring some milk into his coffee with his finger. I can't believe he's here, in my kitchen. It's almost enough to make me forget about the murder, about the way Sophie's mouth was slightly open, a trickle of blood escaping it. Almost.

Zane winks at me. "You look cute in pigtails."

"Thanks," I say, braving a smile.

His eyes are so deep and blue, I could get lost in them.

———

An hour later, I'm sprawled on the couch, clutching my coffee, and Zane is lazily sipping his own drink only inches away. I can see his knee through a large rip in his jeans. The hair on his legs is fine and blond, just like the hair on his head. I fight the urge to reach over and stroke it.

"So you used to live in Iowa City?" I try to make my voice sound sexy and throaty, but it actually comes out kind of squeaky.

"Yeah. I was born here. Moved to Chicago when I was little. Mom wanted to come back. No offense, but I'm not a big fan of Iowa." He smiles apologetically. His teeth are so white. Light blond stubble covers his square jaw. I want to feel it against my cheek, my lips. My proximity to him seems to have narrowed my focus, and all I can see is his face.

"Not many people are," I reply.

Zane picks up a picture of me, my sister, and my dad.

"What does your dad do?" He gestures to the photo.

"He's a pediatric surgeon," I say. "Today he's operating on some kid who was born with his bowels on the outside."

Zane shakes his head. "That's pretty impressive. I mean, your dad's job, not the baby with the guts on the outside."

"I know," I say, a hint of bitterness in my words.

"How about your mom?" We both look down at the picture in his hands, at the space where a mother should be, but isn't.

I'm a little surprised he'd be so bold to ask such a question when it's clear my mom is either dead or off somewhere else, leading a life that doesn't include me, but I remember him on his first day, telling me that his father was dead. It feels like a natural course for our conversation.

"Pancreatic cancer. She died when I was eleven."

He nods, as though I've confirmed what he'd suspected. "That's gotta be rough on a kid."

I peer into my coffee cup. "It was. I mean, it still is. It doesn't help that my dad is gone all the time. I've pretty much become my sister's parent. He didn't even come home to help take care of her when we found out about Sophie's death."

He makes a sympathetic noise. "I know what you mean. My mom hasn't really been herself in years. Ever since my father died, she's been living in her own little world."

"So how old were you when your father died?"

"He killed himself when I was three." The matter-of-fact way he says it shocks me into silence.

"It's cool," Zane says, as if to reassure me that there's no right response to that news. "I don't really remember him. I was too young. I've got this picture of us, though—of him and me. He was pushing me on the swing. And he's smiling really big with his mouth, but you can see in his eyes—he's not happy. He did it about a month after that picture was taken."

Oh god. I wish I could undo this conversation, go back to the dreamy, wispy cloud I was floating on only moments before.

My shyness has been torn away by the revelations that passed between us. I reach out and take his hand, lace my fingers into the spaces between his. His hand grasps mine.

He sets his cup down and turns his head toward me. His breath is sweet despite the coffee, but it's laced with something else—something like sorrow. He presses his lips to my mouth.

Here's the thing about the kiss. It's full of everything I've been missing for so long. Connection. Understanding. Warmth. And it rushes through me so fast, I feel like I'm drowning. I can't breathe. Without thinking, I push him away. His eyes fill with hurt.

Immediately, I regret it. I open my mouth to apologize, but he's already standing up.

"I've gotta go."

He's gone before I can protest. I melt onto the couch,

gasping, realizing I've never wanted anything as much as I want to rewind time and return to that kiss. And it scares me. The fact that something so beautiful and tenuous is within my grasp terrifies me because I know that, at some point, I will just end up losing it.

———

Hours later, I flip through the channels, trying to find something interesting enough to keep me awake until Mattie gets home. I should go upstairs and find my caffeine pills, but I feel stuck, like I've been glued to the couch. It would take way too much energy to climb the stairs. No, I'll just sit here and watch TV and wait.

Hoarders? No.

Full House? No.

The Real World? NO.

I settle on the Science Channel. There's some program about how the world is going to end soon, and it kind of cheers me up because then at least I won't be sliced to bits by Sophie's killer. The show's narrator has such a soothing voice. I find myself succumbing to the sleep I've been staving off for so long. Finally, I just give in.

And promptly slide.

———

Black leather. The vibrations of a running engine travel up my legs and into my spine. I recognize the unmistakable mixture of gasoline and orange shampoo.

Scotch.

But I don't think I'm *inside* Scotch. No. Whoever I've become is sitting in the passenger seat, rubbing her earlobe between her thumb and forefinger. When I realize the girl is missing an earring, I put two and two together. Amber. The damn earring I picked up in the bathroom must have poked through my jeans and touched my thigh.

When Amber turns her head, I see Scotch staring out the windshield into nothingness. The view stretches on for miles and miles. Angled roofs and shedding trees and glowing streetlights. I've been here before, to Lookout Peak. Rollins and I came here the one and only time I smoked pot. We were a total cliché, lying on the hood of his car, staring at the stars and wondering if there was something, anything else out there in the big, starry sky.

"You can't tell anyone," Scotch says.

It seems I've come into the middle of a conversation.

"It was just the one time. We used protection." Desperation tinges Scotch's voice, and I'm sure he's talking about the pregnancy. "The baby probably wasn't even mine. Samantha said she saw Sophie riding around with Mr. Golden after school. Who knows how many guys she was sleeping with?"

Finally, Amber speaks. "When did you find out about the pregnancy?"

"Last week. Before . . ." He doesn't finish his sentence, just takes a swig from a bottle he's been holding between his knees.

Fresh tears spill down Amber's cheeks. I wonder how she ended up here, in Scotch's car, parked at Lookout Peak.

Did she run into him after the funeral? Did he ask her if she wanted to go for a ride? My guess is they were two comets traveling at high velocities when they came crashing together—Scotch drunk, and Amber needing someone to just be with her.

"Do you think that's why she did it?" Amber asks.

Scotch beats his hand on the steering wheel. "I don't know. At first, she talked about taking care of it, going somewhere. But then she said she didn't know if she could go through with it. She just should've gotten rid of it."

I wish I could climb into his brain and pick apart his thoughts. When Sophie told him about the pregnancy, did he panic? Did he insist she get an abortion? Did she refuse?

Even if I did manage to slide into Scotch, I wouldn't be able to read his thoughts. That's not the way sliding works. I'd only see the world from his perspective, and that is *not* an attractive possibility for me.

Amber crosses her arms over her stomach and rocks back and forth.

"It would have ruined my plans. It would have ruined my life."

Scotch takes another pull off the bottle and then shakes his head like it burns going down. He leans toward Amber and starts to nuzzle her neck. She exhales, a cross between a sigh and a moan. When his hand slithers into her lap, I realize where this is going. Memories come rushing back, and instead of being inside the cramped front seat of a Mustang, I'm lying on a bench in the boys' locker room. As Scotch touches Amber, I feel sick, like

I'm witnessing exactly what he did to me that night. It is so, so messed up.

Amber's body responds to Scotch's caresses, and she leans toward him. I'm no longer worried for her safety. I'm worried about my own sanity. If I stay here while they do this, I will surely go insane. Slowly, I feel myself slipping away.

———

Relief rushes through me when I realize I'm back in my own living room. My heart is thumping hard inside my rib cage, and the memories of the homecoming dance last year are rattling my brain. Instead of the program about the impending apocalypse, there's a show about the mating ritual of the baboon. I grab the remote and turn the television off, shuddering.

I take the steps two at a time, unable to get to my room fast enough. Unable to get to my *pills* fast enough. I snatch up my backpack and thrust my hand inside, searching for the familiar curve of the bottle. The childproof top comes off with a twist, and then the white ovals are in my palm, and then they are in my mouth. I swallow them without water, without hesitation.

Only when I feel them sliding down my throat does my heart slow down to a normal rhythm. I vow not to let my guard down again. When my body sinks into the loose-ness of sleep, I leave myself unprotected. I'd rather not sleep at all than be sucked into the presence of would-be rapists. Of killers.

All that night, I lie on my bed and watch old episodes of *Buffy the Vampire Slayer* on Netflix. I imagine myself with a stake, chasing after a shadowy figure in a mask carrying a knife wet with Sophie's blood. I tackle him to the ground and rip away the material obscuring his face. It is Scotch. I raise the stake high and plunge it deep into his chest. He disintegrates like dust and is swallowed up by the earth.

CHAPTER FOURTEEN

In the morning, I take an eternity-long shower, trying to scrub away any remaining bit of Scotch with my vanilla body wash. I'd probably stand here all day, letting the warm water cascade over my body, if my sister didn't scream at me to hurry the hell up. I wrap myself in a frayed brown towel and open the door.

"It's about freaking time," she says. I ignore her and go into my room, pull on some faded jeans and a Minnie Mouse T-shirt, and wrangle a comb through the pink mop on my head, uttering a chain of obscenities. Before me, in the mirror, a girl stares at me with circles under her eyes.

In the kitchen, I find a note from my father: *Early meeting. See you tonight.* I have to admit, I'm a little relieved to miss him. He'd notice the circles and demand to know if I've been taking my Provigil like a good little narcoleptic, and I'm not sure I'd have the strength to lie.

I'm grabbing a brown sugar cinnamon Pop-Tart and stuffing it into my bag when, through the kitchen window,

I see Samantha pull up. Mattie rushes in, grabs a mottled banana, and bolts out, yelling something about being late for practice. Tires squeal as Samantha pulls away.

If I'm going to walk, I'd better hurry up, too. I grab my purple coat from the coat-tree in the front hall and wiggle into it before hurrying out the door.

In my driveway, Zane leans against a white Grand Am. His blond hair is all over the place, and he looks like he hasn't slept.

"Hi," I say, suddenly self-conscious about my appearance. I wish I'd spent some time putting on makeup. At least some concealer to cover the darkness under my eyes.

"Hey. I thought you might need a ride. You don't have a car, right?" His gaze sweeps the driveway.

"No." I plod down the driveway toward him. "I mean, no, I don't have a car. So a ride would be really nice. Thanks."

He holds the door for me and then circles around to the driver's side. My feet brush against crumpled Big Gulp cups and Snickers wrappers. When he turns the key in the ignition, a Nirvana song nearly pops my eardrums. He spins the knob to the left until the song blasts at a more acceptable level.

"Sorry."

"I'm sorry, too," I blurt out, then clamp my hand over my mouth. *Idiot.*

"For what?" He looks bewildered.

"For pushing you away. I was just surprised, that's all."

He stares into his lap. "Well, I shouldn't have kissed

you. We barely know each other." He backs out of my driveway, pausing to glance both ways before pulling into the street.

I want to say the kiss wasn't a mistake. I want to tell him I enjoyed it. I want to tell him I like him so much it terrifies me. Instead, I say, "So, you're into Nirvana?"

"Oh, yeah. Kurt Cobain is, like, my idol."

"Except for the whole killing himself thing, right?"

I mean it to be a joke, but then I remember about his father.

"Oh my god. I'm so sorry. I didn't mean . . ." My voice trails off.

We're both quiet for the five minutes it takes to get to school. Kurt Cobain carries on the conversation for us.

———

We make it to English about thirty seconds before the bell rings. There's something odd about the room. I realize what's strange—Mrs. Winger is standing at the front of the room, smiling at everyone, ready to start the day, rather than huddled in front of her computer playing solitaire.

She's excited about something. She squawks and waves her flabby arms as she explains our assignment. She feels we're in need of some healing after our heartbreaking loss. We need to talk about our feelings, get it all out, some hippy-dippy bullshit. We'll do it anonymously. She passes out green sheets of paper, each one with a code word written at the top. Mine is *yellow*. I sneak a look at my neighbors' papers. *Purple. Black.*

Really working herself up, Mrs. Winger babbles on about the importance of expressing ourselves. She wants us to write what we're feeling now, right this minute. She wants us to pour ourselves out onto the page. Mike Jones raises his hand and asks if "tired" counts as a feeling. She gives him her patented death stare and then continues with her ridiculous monologue.

After we've purged our thoughts and emotions, Mrs. Winger will collect the pages and mix them up. Then she'll randomly pass out the papers, and we'll each write a heartfelt, kind, human response. She has the code words, she warns, so don't even think about writing something mean. She crouches down by Zane's desk, and I hear her tell him that since he's new and didn't know Sophie, he can write about whatever strikes him.

She puts on some classical "writing" music and settles behind her desk, firing up her computer—probably to get some solid solitaire time in—and puts up her feet. We all quietly stare at our papers for a while. Finally, one by one, my classmates bend over their desks and start writing. Zane writes a word, then pauses, writes another. Samantha is hunched over her desk, scribbling furiously.

I'm the last one to begin. My pencil feels strange and hard and it kind of hurts to hold on to. I realize it's because I'm squeezing it so tightly. What do I have to say about Sophie? What am I feeling?

Sophie was one of the nicest people I've ever known.

I pause. It seems wrong to just leave it at *nice. Nice* is

what you say when a stranger asks about your weekend and you don't really want to go into it. *Nice* is the weather. It means nothing. Nothing at all.

What do I really have to say about Sophie?

I chew on my eraser. This *is* anonymous, after all. I flip over my pencil and rub out the part about her being nice.

Sophie was a beautiful person, inside and out, but everyone treated her like crap. The girls she called friends only accepted her when she was skinny. The guy she liked screwed her over. There is more to Sophie's death than you'll ever know.

Before I can write more, Mrs. Winger is at the front of the room, announcing, "Time's up! Fold your papers and turn them in!" I press my paper neatly in half and pass it forward. Once Mrs. Winger has collected all the papers, she shuffles them and then weaves her way among the desks, giving them to new people.

She flips a paper onto my desk. I don't touch it.

When she's finished, she gestures for us to unfold the papers. "Read and respond," she says. "Really connect with each other."

Teachers are so lame. They think they can make us bare our souls through some stupid activity in class. If social boundaries can keep a jock from saying *what's up* to a nerd in the hallway, does she really think in one period she can make us best friends like the kids in *The Breakfast Club*? I roll my eyes and unfold my paper.

There's this girl. And I'm pretty sure I like her. I mean, I know I do, but the thing is I don't know how to tell her. I don't really know the protocol for this sort of thing. So yeah. I guess that's all. If you have some advice, it would be greatly appreciated.

I steal a look at Zane. It has to be his. No one else was told to just write about whatever. Is it vain to think he could be writing about me? I remember how his lips felt on mine, so warm and sudden. I wish I could go back to that moment, go with the flow, not ruin it.

"Two-minute warning!" Mrs. Winger is already dancing around, trying to hurry us. Shit. What to say?

Quickly, I jot down, *Tell her she's so pretty it kills you a little.*

Then I refold the piece of paper and push it into Mrs. Winger's waiting hands. She collects the rest of the papers and then starts unfolding them and handing them back according to the code words at the top. I watch Zane open his. He smiles.

She places my paper in front of me. I skim past my original note and read the response: *Uh, I think you're reading too much into this. Girl had problems. She took the easy way out. Done.* I glance around the room. Samantha is watching me carefully. I slowly crumple the piece of paper, holding her gaze the whole time. She looks away.

The bell rings. Zane pauses by my desk, waiting for me to gather my things. On the way out the door, I toss the paper into the garbage can. Zane says something about Mrs. Winger literally having wings when she waves her arms around, and I'm laughing as we turn the corner and enter the hallway.

I catch sight of Rollins, halfway down the hall, heading in our direction, probably to meet up with me. He blinks when he sees me with Zane, and looks a little hurt. I try to smile and wave, but he ducks into a bathroom. My hand flutters uselessly down by my side.

———

Everyone stares as I walk down the hall with Zane. It's probably partly because Zane is the New Kid, and there's always a bit of a mystery shrouding the New Kid, but mostly it's because he is smoking hot. I savor the look of jealousy I get when we pass by a bunch of freshman girls.

Zane stops at the drinking fountain to fill his green Nalgene bottle, and I wait, shifting my books from one hip to the other. The hallway hollows out by the second, people rushing to class before the bell rings.

"What do you have next?" I ask when he straightens.

"Government with Carson. Guess I could use a nap."

Mr. Carson has to be over a hundred years old. He's been teaching here since our school opened in the 1950s. His idea of a lesson plan is ordering you to copy five pages of messily scrawled notes from the overhead, lulling you into a nearly comatose state, and then scaring you to death by hacking up a lung into a purple hanky right when you least expect it. Every year, people place bets on whether this'll be his last.

"Oh, come on. His class is *scintillating*." I stress the cheap SAT vocabulary word, and Zane laughs. The sound heats me up.

All morning, I've been imagining Zane's lips pressed to mine, like the image of us kissing is superimposed on reality. We're just standing here in the hallway chatting, but in my head our limbs are wrapped around each other, our bodies doing the talking.

The bell rings, threatening reality. I want to escape into an alternate universe, one where I get to make out with Zane beneath the bleachers instead of wondering who killed Sophie Jacobs. Suddenly I understand the presence of that condom wrapper I saw under the bleachers last week. It was evidence of someone breaking away from the homework and lockers and lunch ladies—someone fleeing a world that lets a girl disappear and doesn't ask questions.

"Do you want to skip?" I ask, and the question is so out of nowhere it even surprises *me*.

"And go where?"

"I know a place."

Zane smiles. He doesn't know that *he* is my refuge, the place I will go to escape.

———

It's colder this week. The wind whooshes beneath the bleachers, cutting through the thin material of my T-shirt. I should have thought out this plan better, brought my coat or something. But then Zane shrugs out of one side of his oversized corduroy coat, offering to let me share it with him, and I think everything is perfect.

"So this is your place?" He looks around him, taking it all in. The candy bar wrappers. The cigarette butts. The mounds of dead leaves.

"It's not much," I say. "But yeah. It's where I go."

Zane nods. "It's got a certain . . . mystique to it."

Mystique. Just the word to describe a place where you can see but can't be seen, where you hear the things you don't want to know. Just then, I realize why I'm so comfortable under the bleachers. Me lurking down here, it's just like me sliding. I am a witness. Never a participant.

"Something on your mind?" Zane asks, bumping into me playfully.

There is actually something on my mind. I keep replaying the conversation I heard between Scotch and Amber. The thing he'd said about ruining his plans—would he go so far as to kill Sophie if she didn't get an abortion? Is that too far-fetched?

I feel like I need a new perspective. I could tell Zane the basics without revealing my secret. Maybe he'll have some insight.

"Okay, you know the girl who died? Sophie?"

Zane nods.

"Well, this officer came to our house, asking my sister questions about Sophie's state of mind. He happened to mention Sophie was pregnant when she died."

"Holy shit."

"Yeah. Anyway . . . I think I might know who the father was. You know Scotch Becker?"

Zane groans. "Who could forget a guy named Scotch? He's the charming fellow who suggested I come out after football. He said I seemed cool enough to get some of his castoffs."

I pause, the statement hitting a little close to home. "Gross. Okay, so the day Sophie died, I overheard Scotch telling one of his friends that he slept with Sophie."

Zane stares straight ahead. "That just . . . sucks."

I follow his gaze to the empty field. It's easier to look at nothing when talking about these things than to look into Zane's eyes and try to guess what he's thinking. What I'm about to say might derail everything that's happened between us in the past few days. Maybe he'll think I'm crazy, paranoid like Samantha's note in English class said.

But maybe not.

"Okay, so is it totally insane to think Sophie might not have killed herself?" I continue to not look at Zane. Instead, I pick up an orangey-brown leaf and start to shred it.

A moment passes.

"Um. What do you mean? If she didn't kill herself, then who killed her?"

Another moment.

"You think Scotch killed her? Because of the pregnancy? You think he killed her and made it look like a suicide?" His voice sounds doubtful, but not like he thinks the idea is so out there I must be destined for a padded cell.

"It's a theory," I say diplomatically. "Hey, Scott Peterson killed his wife when she was pregnant. And they were married. Scotch had a lot to lose. He'd probably have to give up his college scholarship and get a job at a car dealership or something. He'd never get out of Iowa."

Zane hunches forward and rubs his chin thoughtfully.

"Yeah, I guess. Still, it seems like a big assumption—that he'd kill a girl over a lost scholarship?"

I could tell Zane about what Scotch did to me freshman year. If I do, though, it's like it turns me into Damaged Girl, and I don't want that. I decide to shoot a different theory his way.

"Okay, here's another possibility. Kids have been talking about Sophie riding around with Mr. Golden. What if he's the father? That would definitely be a motive to kill Sophie, wouldn't it? His job would be at stake. He could go to jail for sleeping with a minor. But if he took her out and made it look like she killed herself, he'd be off the hook."

Zane twists his mouth, like he's considering his words carefully. "Maaaaaaybe. Or maybe she just killed herself, Sylvia. I mean, that's what people do when they feel like there's no escape."

I feel the weight of his father's suicide hanging between us. Zane, more than anyone, would know how each day could burden someone so much that they'd want to take their own life. The thing is, he didn't know Sophie. If he did, maybe he'd be more willing to think outside the box.

"I'm not saying you're wrong, Sylvia. I'm just saying that, when it comes to these things, the least complicated explanation is usually right. Sophie was pregnant. She didn't know what to do. She was probably scared. She felt like she had no way out. Sounds like a recipe for disaster to me."

I have to admit, he makes a good point.

We are quiet for a while, and I just let the heat from his body seep into mine. Sharing his coat reminds me of when Rollins and I pretended to be Siamese twins. Except when I was with Rollins, my heart didn't feel like it was going to slam its way right out of my chest.

I hear a faraway bell. The period has ended. It's time to return to my own personal hell, high school. Zane slips his half of the coat off and puts it around my shoulder, fully enveloping me with warmth.

"Come on," he says. "And try to avoid the broken glass. Can't have you going to the nurse and meeting some other guy."

CHAPTER FIFTEEN

Zane and I mix with the stream of students flowing down the hallway. Someone catches my elbow, and I turn to see a blond cheerleader I used to be sort of friends with. Her eyes are bright, and she's bubbling with excitement.

"You missed it. Mattie and Amber got into a fight!"

"What?"

"Just now. Mattie called Amber a slut, so Amber punched her. It was. So. Insane." The girl breaks away from me and launches herself toward someone else to broadcast the latest news.

"What's wrong?" Zane asks when he sees how white my face has become.

"It's my sister. Jesus, I've gotta find her. I'll talk to you later."

"Sure, no problem. See you." He squeezes my hand and then disappears into the crowd of people. I stand on my tippy-toes and survey the masses on their way to class, frantically searching for my sister's face. She's nowhere to be seen. I let the flow of bodies carry me down the hallway, passing classrooms and drinking fountains. As we pass the office, I spot Mattie through the window.

Mattie and Amber sit outside the principal's office, only one tacky orange chair between them. They avoid looking at each other, grimacing at their laps. My sister's clothes are disheveled, the neckline of her cheerleading uniform ripped.

Nasty emerges from his office. His mouth makes shapes and his finger points as he speaks, but I can't hear him behind the smudgy window. He says something to my sister and then waves her out of his office like he's tired of seeing her.

She bursts through the door and almost slams right into me. "Vee!"

I steer her toward the girls' bathroom by her elbow. A senior in ridiculously high heels stands before a mirror, coaxing a contact lens back into place. She blinks a few times, picks up her pink purse from the counter, and brushes past us on her way out. All the stalls are empty, so I'm free to WTF all I want.

"What happened?" I demand, crossing my arms over my chest.

Promptly, Mattie bursts into tears. "Amber's such a bitch. She said Scotch knocked Sophie up and that's why she killed herself."

I let out a deep breath. "She said that?"

Mattie ducks into a stall and starts unrolling toilet paper. She dabs at her cheeks, wiping away the mascara streams coursing down her face. "Yeah, well, we were at my locker, and Samantha made some comment about Amber taking off with Scotch after the funeral. Amber hinted that he told her something big, and we kind of pushed her into telling us."

"And then she hit you?"

Mattie shakes her head. "No. Amber said that's why Sophie must have killed herself—because of the pregnancy. I got pissed because it's like she was excusing herself from any responsibility. I mean, after what we did . . . So I asked her if she'd already forgotten about the picture we'd sent everyone, if she really thought that had nothing to do with Sophie's suicide. That's when she punched me."

I sigh. "Say no more."

Mattie dissolves into tears. I can't stand the way she's crying, knowing she blames herself for Sophie's death. I want so badly to tell her that, although Sophie was unbearably hurt by her friends' actions, she didn't kill herself. I can't bring myself to tell her the truth, and I hate myself for it.

Instead, I pull her close and wrap my arms around her. "Mattie, you can't blame yourself or Amber for Sophie's death. There were other factors involved. Trust me. If you want to feel bad about making a mistake, go ahead, but make it a productive feeling. Don't do anything like that again. But you *can't* go around thinking Sophie is dead because of you."

Mattie pulls away slightly and looks me in the eyes. "Are you sure?"

"Of course I am, Mattie. I swear. You have to trust me."

She leans her head on my shoulder and sniffles. "I do."

After a moment, she pulls away and goes to the sink. She splashes water on her face and then smooths her hair. Meeting my gaze in the mirror, she offers a small smile. "Thanks, Vee."

"No problem. So what did Nasty say?"

"He went easy on me because of Sophie's death. He said he knew I was going through a lot, so he only gave me three days of in-school suspension. I'm supposed to go around and get stuff to work on."

In-school suspension is so *not* a big deal. Kids call it lockup, ironically. You have to sit in a little room attached to the teachers' lounge and listen to the teachers gossip about who's screwing who and who cheated on the *Macbeth* final exam. There's a pop machine right outside the door, and if you play your cards right, you can nab a can of soda to make your stay more enjoyable. Not that I would know or anything.

Mattie's skin is all blotchy, and her eyes are red and puffy. A red welt is forming on her cheek, where I assume Amber hit her. She looks like she's about to start crying again any minute.

"Look, do you want me to go around and get your assignments for you?"

"Would you?" she asks hopefully. "I don't want anyone to see me."

"Sure. I'm not exactly in the mood for class." To be completely truthful, I'm not exactly in the mood to run into Rollins after he snubbed me this morning.

She pounces on me. "You're the best!"

I walk her to the teachers' lounge. The window is covered in newspaper—probably so we can't see the teachers partying during their prep periods. Mattie waves and ducks into the lounge. After she disappears, I try to figure out which of her classes to go to first. I decide to hit up her English class, since it's the closest. Her teacher isn't all that excited that I interrupted class, but she finds a *Romeo and Juliet* study guide and shoves it my way. Mattie's other teachers are more pleasant and give me some worksheets to pass on to her.

Next, I stop by her locker to get her textbooks. You can open 97.3 percent of the lockers at City High by punching them in just the right spot, so you learn really quickly to carry all valuables with you. Mattie's locker, which she shared with Sophie, is a disaster. Photos are taped haphazardly on the inside of the door, among scribbled messages saying things like "Scotch is hawt" and "Mattie + Sophie = BFFEE" (Best Friends For-Effing-Ever).

My eyes fall on one picture in the center of everything, the eye of the storm. Mattie stands between Sophie and Amber, and their arms are all around each other's waists. From the way their faces are painted like cats, I can tell it's from the state fair last summer. It seems like the picture was taken a million years ago. One of the girls is now dead, and the other two just mauled each other in the hallway. It reminds me how quickly things can change.

On the bottom of her locker, under her gym shoes that

smell like rotting broccoli, under a bunch of flyers advertising the cheerleaders' car wash from September, under something suspiciously slimy in a paper bag, I find Mattie's English textbook. I shake my head and pull it out, feeling a bit like the magician who snatches a tablecloth out from under a bunch of china.

As I straighten up, I see Amber headed my way. Her hair hangs in long, messy clumps, and it's pretty clear she's been crying. It's actually really sad. Between witnessing her crumpled on the bathroom floor of a funeral home and then later making out with Scotch Becker, the lowest of the low, I only feel pity for her.

She stops at her locker and spins the knob. When she tries to pull the locker open, nothing happens. She tries again. And again. The locker stays shut. Finally, she releases a shriek and pounds on the metal before drooping in defeat.

"Amber?"

She turns her miserable face toward me.

"Are you okay? Do you want some help?"

She laughs bitterly. "I want a lot of things. Can you turn back time for me? Because that'd be great. I could go back and not be such an idiot. Not send that picture to everyone. Not be such a slut. Not get into a huge fight with my best friend." She shakes her head.

"I meant with your locker." I push past her gently and pound on the door in just the right spot. It pops open.

"Thanks," she mutters, and pulls out her backpack. She shrugs it over her shoulders and slams the locker door. "Guess I'll see ya later."

I watch her walk down the hallway and disappear around the corner.

Maybe I've been wrong about Amber all along. Beneath that cold, bitchy exterior, it seems like she's actually pretty vulnerable. She's able to see the error of her ways, at least, and that's more than you can say for some people. Once Mattie's cooled off, I vow to put in a good word for Amber. They can help each other get past Sophie's death.

Armed with the English textbook and work sheets, I head toward the teachers' lounge. In the detention room, Mattie is sitting with her back to the door, her head cradled in her arms. At first, I wonder if she's crying, but when I touch her back and she turns toward me, her eyes are clear.

I set the work sheets and textbook on the desk in front of her.

"Thanks," she says.

"No problem," I reply. "You'd do the same for me." In my head, though, I'm wondering if it's true.

When I turn to leave, Mattie grabs my arm.

"No, really," she says. "I appreciate you being here for me. I know we haven't always gotten along . . ."

"Don't worry about it. That's what I'm here for." I mean what I say, but as I turn to leave, I find myself wondering who *I'm* supposed to count on.

CHAPTER SIXTEEN

After school, I fight my way through the crowd to get to my locker. It seems like everyone is yapping about the fight. I wish I had earplugs so I could stop hearing all the gossip about my sister and Amber.

Just as I'm stuffing an orange notebook into the already-bursting seams of my poor bag, Rollins appears. He leans on the locker next to mine.

"Hey. I heard about your sister. That sucks."

I give him a cold look. There's something about him ignoring me this morning and now trying to act all buddy-buddy with me that rubs me the wrong way.

"So we're friends now? Because I wasn't sure after this morning . . ."

"What are you talking about?" Rollins tries to look innocent. It's infuriating.

I feel like everything from the last couple of days is building up inside me, a crescendo of terror and anger and frustration. The need for release is so strong.

I turn to face him. "Let's review. You walk out on Friday

night for no reason. When my sister's best friend dies, you don't call. You don't text. Nothing. And now you're avoiding me in the halls. Oh, yeah. I saw you this morning. As soon as you realized I was with Zane, you turned and walked away. Let me tell you something, Rollins. I need a friend right now. Get it?"

A muscle in his jaw twitches. He doesn't say a word, just does a 180 and walks the other way, his fists clenching and unclenching.

"What was that all about?"

Zane pops out of nowhere and stoops down to rest his arm on my open locker door. His grin is a mile wide—so bright and warm, I can almost feel the sun beating down on my face.

"Nothing," I mutter. "I'm just having a really heinous day."

"Hmmm," he says, pressing one finger against his chin like he's thinking hard. "There's only one thing that makes me feel better when I'm having a bad day. Jelly doughnuts."

"What?" My stony face cracks into a smile.

"Jelly doughnuts. They're like an instant orgasm for your tongue. Come on, we'll go get some. I know the best place."

I slam my locker door and let him lead me down the hall toward the parking lot.

——

An hour and 89,467 calories later, we pull into my driveway. I'm still licking the cherry goodness from my fingers, sighing from the clump of sugar in my belly. The air in the car is sweet and comfortably warm.

"Can I ask you a question?" Zane says, playing with the radio. He puts on some bad eighties music. It's perfect.

"Go for it."

"Rollins and you, you're tight?"

"We're friends," I say, and then start to feel pretty guilty about blowing up at Rollins. To make up for it, I add, "*Best* friends."

Zane absorbs this information. "I keep thinking about yesterday." His hand is on the armrest between us, not far away from my bare arm. Goose bumps. "I'm sorry I kissed you so soon. I feel like I ruined everything. I mean, I think you're really interesting. I'd like to get to know you better."

A feeling like happiness swirls beneath my skin. He wants to get to know me better. That means he doesn't think I'm a crazy bitch for throwing out those murder theories, right? That means he feels this connection, too.

"It's just a really weird time for me," I say finally. "With this whole Sophie thing and my sister freaking out. I feel like I'm stuck in this nightmare and everyone's insane but me. Or maybe I'm the one who's insane. I don't know."

Shut up, Vee. Shut up. You're babbling.

After a while, he says softly, "I had a little sister once."

We are both quiet. Even though the heater is blasting hot air right in my face, I feel cold from the tips of my toes to the top of my scalp. The way he said it, in past tense, makes me feel like crying.

"I'm sorry," I say, and then I wish I had said something

else, anything else. "Do you want to talk about it?"

He squeezes his eyes shut and shakes his head.

The white bag I'm holding between my thighs crinkles as I pull out a pastry. "Jelly doughnut?"

Our eyes meet, and he shines his smile again. It warms me up fast. His fingers brush mine as he takes the doughnut from me. He takes a big bite, chews, swallows.

"God," he says. "You're so pretty. It just kills me."

"It was you," I whisper. "In class, I mean. That *was* your note."

His lips bend into a smile.

The moment freezes. And right now, I don't care if this will end someday. My fear of becoming too attached is swept away by my intense desire to make this instant count, make it as complete as it can be.

My hand floats up to his face and touches his cheek. Leaning toward each other, we kiss, ever so gently. His lips taste like cherry. I didn't know it could be this good.

———

When I manage to extricate myself from Zane's car, I notice my dad's car is in the driveway—an odd sight in the middle of the day. I thought he was going to be at the hospital, catching up on some paperwork.

Once inside, I set down my backpack and head to the kitchen to get a drink of water. A strange sound makes me pause in the middle of the foyer. It's a rustling—no, it's someone whispering. The noise is coming from my father's study. I inch closer, straining to hear what's being said.

"Just stop," my father hisses loudly. "I told you. Please don't call anymore." A moment passes, and then he says, "No. I'm done. Goodbye."

I'm frozen. I know I should turn around, go to the kitchen for a glass of water like I planned, but my muscles will not obey my command. Who could my father have been talking to? It sounded like he was putting an end to some sort of relationship. But he hasn't gone out on any dates . . . has he?

My father appears in the doorway with his cell phone, and his face looks older than it normally does. Deep creases carve into his face around his eyes and mouth. His back is hunched over. He looks up, surprised to see me.

"Vee," he says. "How long have you been standing there?"

I shrug, trying to appear casual. "Not long."

He slips his cell phone into his pocket and grabs his jacket. "I've got to run to the store for a few things. You need me to pick anything up?"

"No," I say.

"Okay. I won't be long."

And then he's gone.

I linger in the doorway of his office, trying to make sense of the phone call I overheard. I have to admit, I kind of always pictured my dad staying single for the rest of his life. It had never occurred to me that he'd want to see anyone after my mom died.

On his desk, a framed photo of my mother grabs my attention. It's from their wedding. In it, she smiles widely at the camera, as if she's got her whole life ahead of her, as if nothing bad could ever happen. As if she could never die, as if my father could never love anyone but her.

Looking at it makes me feel heavy with sadness. Only moments ago, I was kissing a gorgeous boy, maybe even falling a little bit in love. I was throwing caution to the wind, letting myself get stuck to something. But right now, in front of me, is the evidence that all good things, no matter how beautiful, come to an end.

I turn around and trudge up the stairs, my heart weighing me down.

CHAPTER SEVENTEEN

Dinner is awkward.

Mattie sits there, twisting her spoon in her hands, avoiding eye contact with my dad. He fills our bowls with steaming chili and places them in front us silently. The chili is his way of making amends for not being around when Mattie's dealing with her best friend's death and for relying on me to pick up the slack. I also wonder if he's making up for something else, maybe for not being entirely truthful with us. For keeping his relationship with whoever was on the phone earlier on the down-low.

He reaches across the table for some saltines to crumble into his chili and then asks casually—almost *too* casually, "So what happened with Amber today, Mattie?"

Mattie stares intently at the spoon in her fist.

"She was saying some stuff about Sophie."

"What *kind* of stuff?" He takes a bite, chews methodically, never looking away from Mattie's face.

After a long pause, Mattie says, "She was saying Sophie was pregnant with Scotch Becker's baby."

My father swallows, frowns. "And why would that upset you?"

Mattie drums her spoon on the table. "Because she said that's why Sophie killed herself, and I know that's not true."

"So you hit her?"

Mattie lets her spoon fall to the table. "I didn't hit her! She hit me. I just called her a name. I shouldn't have been *suspended* for that."

My dad keeps his cool. "Well, Mr. Nast can't just allow kids to get into brawls in the hallway. He has a school to run. There have to be consequences, even if—"

"Even if what?" Mattie says, looking him in the eyes, challenging him.

"Even if you're hurting."

Mattie lets out a long breath. "You have *no* idea." She then picks up her untouched bowl of chili and heads for the kitchen. I hear the dish hit the sink with a great deal of force. My dad winces.

"I'm going to bed," Mattie announces on her way back through the dining room. She stomps up the stairs and slams her bedroom door.

My dad sighs and puts his head in his hands.

I desperately want to follow Mattie's lead and bow out of this whole depressing family meal, but it seems cruel to let my father sit there by himself. When he raises his head, I see the tears glistening in his eyes.

"I can't do this by myself," he says, more to the ceiling than to me. I'm not sure how to respond. I'm not sure if I *should* respond.

"God. If only your mother were here," he goes on. "I'm just . . . unequipped. I can't deal with this."

His yearning for my mother sinks into me. In that moment, I almost wish he *was* seeing someone. He needs someone in his life besides me and Mattie—someone to talk to.

I reach over and link my hand with his. "You're doing fine, Dad. Mattie's just upset. She'll be okay." I hope what I'm saying isn't a lie.

He looks at our hands, intertwined, and a tear comes loose and spills down his cheek. He squeezes my hand and attempts a smile. "You remind me so much of your mother sometimes, Vee. She always knew just what to say. It was like she could look inside of you and know exactly what you were feeling. You're like that."

His words make me a little uncomfortable. Usually I feel like I know *too much* about other people—their secrets eat away at me from the inside.

"Vee. Would you do me a favor? Go to your sister. She needs help. You probably understand what she's going through more than I ever could. You'll know the right things to say."

I manage a small smile. "Sure, Dad."

My father's phone buzzes. He pulls it out of his pocket, glances at the display, and answers it. "Hello?" As I watch, his eyes dry up and become businesslike. "No problem. I'll be there in a half hour."

He hangs up and looks at me. "I'm sorry, Vee. I have to go."

"I know," I reply. "Go."

Upstairs, Mattie is lying on her bed, flipping through a photo album of happier times. On one page, my mother pushes me on a swing, and my sister is visible in the background, strapped into a pink stroller. She's reaching her arms out, like she longs to join in on the fun. The next page shows my mom and dad cooking dinner together. I am dancing between them, tasting something on a wooden spoon and making a face. She is stuck in her highchair, a mound of cereal on her tray.

I sit next to her on the bed, but she doesn't look up. She says her words to the people in the pictures. "What do you remember about her?" She traces her finger over our mother's smile.

"About Mom?"

Mattie nods. "I feel like I've forgotten everything important."

I flop back on the bed and stare at the ceiling. "I don't know. She smelled like violets. When we went on car trips, she made up stories about the constellations in the sky. They were like people to her. They all had pasts and relationships and mannerisms. She could go on for hours about the Gemini twins fighting over Andromeda."

Mattie turns the page. "What else?"

"She ate peanut butter and banana sandwiches. She played her music loud and jumped around. She painted her toenails purple."

Mattie examines each page in the photo album carefully, as if she's looking for clues about who our mother was. When she reaches the final page, it's blank. It's always been blank. I don't know what she was expecting. She hurls the book to the floor.

"It's not enough," she says, her words strangled by her sobs.

I sit up and wrap my arms around her. "I know," I whisper. "I know it's not enough. But listen. We've got each other. If you need to talk about something, you can tell me. Anything, okay?"

Mattie nods and grabs a tissue from her bedside table. I rub her back as she blows her nose. The light outside has gone dim. We are surrounded by shadows.

Eventually, my sister pulls away and rearranges herself on the bed, hugging a pillow across her chest. "Can I ask you a question, Vee?"

"Yeah."

She picks some lint off the pillow. "Why did you stop being friends with Sam and all those guys?"

I sigh. I'd been content to let Mattie think the popular crowd rejected me just for being a geek, but the way she looks at me makes me want to tell her the truth—or at least as much of it as I can. Besides, she should know what the people she hangs around with are capable of. Maybe it will save her from putting herself in the same situation I did.

"Do you remember the purple dress?" I ask.

She bobs her head excitedly, like I knew she would. She was there when I found the dress. She was almost more excited about it than I was.

And so I tell her.

I tell her about me and Samantha both liking Scotch. I tell her I was the one he chose and about all the things Samantha did to punish me for that. I tell her about drinking in Kapler Park before the dance. I tell her about how I felt ill and passed out, and how I awoke with my dress around my waist, to the sound of Rollins's fists hitting Scotch's body.

The only part I leave out is the sliding, but let's face it—it's not necessary to the story. What happened that night could happen to anyone. It is not a unique story. But it is enough to cause my sister's face to screw up again with tears, enough to compel her to throw her arms around me and crush me with her embrace.

It's been a long time since I cried about that night. But for some reason, telling it all to Mattie, I see it from a different angle. My heart swells for the girl in the purple dress, for the girl with a crush who got more than she asked for. As I recall seeing it from Samantha's eyes—Scotch dragging me into the locker room—I start to cry for the girl I once was.

And so I let my sister hug me, and when she asks me to stay in her room tonight, I oblige. It's like when we were little, after my mom died, and she had a nightmare. She'd come into my room, and I'd hold up the covers for her to crawl under.

I watch her face as it settles into sleep. She looks so young, so raw. I'm angry for her that she didn't have more time with our mother, that the only person she really has right now is me. These thoughts circle over my head, and before I know it, I have fallen asleep.

I'm in the middle of a carnival. A Ferris wheel spins backward and a sad clown holds a bunch of black balloons. My mother rides a purple unicorn on the merry-go-round. I see her coming my way, and she waves, her face glowing in excitement. She looks just like her pictures, young and stunning.

She looks like an angel.

I run up to the gate and press against it, calling for her. Someone taps me on the shoulder, and when I turn around, there she is. She wears ripped blue jeans and an Alice in Chains T-shirt.

"Vee," she says, her voice soft and shimmery. She pulls me to a bench, and we sit down, hands clasped. I rest my head against her shoulder, breathing in her mother scent of powder and violets and milk.

"Mom."

It feels good to say the word. I have so many things to ask her. How did she know she was in love with Dad? Did his kisses taste like jelly doughnuts? How do I carry on each day with the knowledge of the terrible things people are capable of? How do I help my sister work through the blackness of one friend's death and another friend's betrayal?

All my questions fall away when I look in her eyes, blue against the black sky.

She pushes my hair back from my face. "My baby."

"Yes. Yes, Mom." I can't stop saying it. "Mom."

The rain begins to fall, and each drop that slides down my mother's cheeks takes away a tiny bit of her. She hugs me one last time, and then the rain picks up and takes her away entirely. The rain takes away everything.

I am crying when I awake in Mattie's room. How unfair is this, to be given a mother for a few seconds in a dream, only to have her be taken away the moment I open my eyes. The pillow is wet with tears.

The alarm clock says it's a little past ten. I need to get up, do something that will keep me alert. I slither out of Mattie's bed and tiptoe to the hallway, leaving her door just slightly ajar.

In my room, I snap on the light, and brightness blinds me. A face captures my attention in the corner of the room, but when I look, I realize it's only the face of the angel on the Smashing Pumpkins T-shirt. I'd hung the shirt over the back of my rocking chair and forgotten it. Something about the angel's eyes, the expression on her face. It reminds me of my mother.

Drawn to the shirt, I thread my arms through the sleeves and pull it over my head. It's softer than it looks, but its caress on my skin is a poor substitute for my dream mother's embrace.

After popping a few caffeine pills, I retrieve the astronomy book from my nightstand. I flip it open to a random page and start reading about the big bang theory. After only a paragraph, the words start to swerve on the page.

Dizziness. A slight pain behind my eyes.

I'm going to slide.

And then I realize I'm wearing the shirt that Rollins gave me.

An entire field pops up around me—not a natural field, but a man-made field, complete with white paint marking the perimeters for playing football. I see the dark but unmistakable outline of the school. Beyond it, the black sky sings with stars.

Rollins crosses the field, heading in the direction of a goalpost. It is strange to be inside him. The way his body moves, his kind of slouchy walk, is so familiar to me—but I've never experienced it from this perspective. I don't know how I've avoided it in the year that I've known him. I used to think it was because he contained his feelings so well. He never left an emotional imprint on anything.

Except the T-shirt he gave me. How strange.

As he approaches the goalpost, I see the silhouette of someone waiting for him—a female silhouette. I'm surprised by a sudden pang of jealousy. I didn't know he was seeing anyone. Have we drifted so far apart that I wouldn't know these things?

The girl's hair shines in the dim light coming from the faraway streetlamp. I only know one girl with that exact chocolate brown. It is Amber. Amber Prescott.

Confusion overwhelms me. Though Amber has never made her attraction to Rollins a secret, he always brushes her off. What is going on here?

When he's about five yards away, I hear him say, "Thanks for coming."

Amber smiles and reaches into the black-and-white Prada purse that's slung over her shoulder. She pulls out a crumply packet, but it's too dark for me to tell what it is.

"I'm glad you called. I was feeling a little lonely."

Rollins opens his mouth to respond, but I'm snatched away before I can hear what he says. I jolt upright and gasp for air. I pull off the Smashing Pumpkins T-shirt and chuck it on the floor.

———

My phone wakes me before dawn. I sit up, feeling blindly for it. I must have fallen asleep in the early morning hours, despite the handful of caffeine pills I gulped down after witnessing Rollins's meeting with Amber.

It's my dad's ringtone, the one he made me download last year when I was stressing about finals—"Don't Worry, Be Happy." I swear the song is more annoying than my alarm clock.

"Dad? It's like five thirty."

"Vee, I've got to talk to you."

And, with those words, I know something terrible has happened. It's the kind of thing you say to someone right before breaking bad news. Like telling a child there's no Santa Claus. Or their cat got run over by a truck.

Or something much, much worse.

I'm suddenly sitting up, crushing the phone against my ear.

"What is it?"

"Amber's parents called. She didn't come home last night. They wondered if she was with Mattie." There's more. I can tell by his tone of voice there's something he's not telling me.

"And?"

"Honey, Amber is dead." The stark finality of his words knocks the breath out of me.

I take a moment, struggling to find my voice, trying to remember the last time I saw Amber. It was outside the principal's office. That was the last time I saw her with my *own* eyes.

But I was *with* her around ten p.m. last night.

Or, rather, Rollins was with her.

I switch the phone from one ear to the other.

"Mr. Golden heard the shot and found her body on the football field—isn't that your psychology teacher? Evidently he was at school, preparing lesson plans for the day. God knows why he was there so late. What teacher stays until ten o'clock? The police say . . . it looks like another suicide."

I'm willing to bet it wasn't a suicide. Just like Sophie's death wasn't a suicide.

"Vee, are you okay?" He's making sure I've got my shit together so I can take care of Mattie. What choice do I have? I have to be okay. I have to keep Mattie safe.

Two cheerleaders are dead. She could be next.

"I'll be home by tonight, okay? We've got a bad situation here. I need you to stay with Mattie until I get home. There's no school today. The police have cordoned off the area."

I picture it in my head—yellow tape stretched around the football field, waving in the wind. Chalk marking where the body was found. Can you use chalk on grass?

My father interrupts my thoughts. "Okay? Okay, Vee? Can you handle that?"

I'm nodding, but he can't see it. "Yeah, okay, Dad. Should I tell her?"

I hear him release a deep breath. "I guess you'd better. Will you guys be okay today?" Guilt has crept into his voice. Another traumatic event that he won't be around for.

"Don't worry," I say, and his ringtone pops into my head. *Be happy.* "I'll take care of everything."

CHAPTER EIGHTEEN

In the kitchen, I mix pancake batter while thinking of what I'll say to Mattie. There seems no good way to tell her. I'm glad I'm not a doctor. My father must go through this all the time, searching his mind for the perfect words to break bad news. I wonder why he's not better at it. Maybe I should be thinking about what my mother would say if she were here.

I pour little circles of batter into a sizzling pan, then grab a handful of chocolate chips and drop them one by one into the pancakes. A knock at the door startles me. I peer through the window and see Rollins standing on our porch. I freeze for a moment and then duck down before he can see me. It's not something I think about, just instinct. Try as I might, I can't come up with a way to explain how Amber died right after she met up with Rollins.

He knocks again. I close my eyes.

Go. Away.

After about five minutes, I pick myself up off the floor and peek out the window. The porch is empty. Rollins is gone. I heave a sigh of relief.

I scoop the pancakes onto a plate. I spend a long time standing in front of the refrigerator, looking at a picture of my mom when she was in college, tan and skinny and smiling, with blond hair and a white tank top. Below it, there's a picture of my sister at her eighth-grade graduation. Dad and I stand on either side of her, giving her double bunny ears. On any other fridge, this would look like a happy collage of memories, but on our fridge it's a mockery of what once was, what could have been. A happy family.

I pull the refrigerator door open and grab the syrup so I can drizzle it on my sister's pancakes, just the way she likes them.

———

I nudge Mattie's door open with my foot and carry in the tray of pancakes and orange slices. Now that I'm standing there, it seems silly, like pancakes could possibly soften the blow that another of her friends is dead. I'm acting just like my freaking dad. Taking a couple of steps backward, I rest the tray on the floor in the hall and then enter the room again. I will do this in my own way.

She's snoring, her eyelashes thick against her cheeks. The strangest urge creeps through me—to crawl into bed next to her, wrap my arms around her, feel her torso rise and fall with each breath. Instead, I open the curtains and let the sun shine in, hoping it will obliterate the darkness my news will bring.

"Mattie?" I sit down next to her, shaking her gently. "Mattie, wake up."

She opens one eye and studies me. Then she jerks upright, throwing her princess-pink covers away from her body.

"What time is it? Oh my God, I'm going to be late for practice. What—do I smell pancakes? Is it Sunday?" She stares at me, confused.

"Mattie, I have something to tell you."

She freezes, a look of apprehension washing over her face. Her muscles tense, like she's bracing herself for the impact.

"There's no school today. Amber's dead." No euphemisms, just the bald, ugly words. I rip the Band-Aid off and wait for her to scream.

Mattie's shoulders droop, then her eyes. I see the knowledge working its way through every muscle group, as they all become slack. First, her face. Then her arms. Then the trunk of her body. She slumps there, devoid of any expression at all.

"They found her on the football field. They think it was suicide." Even as I'm speaking, I'm not entirely sure who *they* are. I have a vague mental picture of Officer Teahen and a bunch of uniformed figures inching their way across the campus, looking for clues.

Mattie says nothing.

I'm afraid to leave her alone, so I go into my room and grab some CDs and my old teddy bear, Cleo. I pop my Smashing Pumpkins CD into Mattie's computer because that's what I like to listen to when I feel as if my life is being sucked out of me. Billy Corgan's voice is a salve.

Pushing Cleo into her hands, I say, "Mattie? You're

going to get through this. I promise." Then I climb into bed and wrap my arms around her, pretending we're stranded in Antarctica and I have to use my body heat to keep her alive. Strangely, it's only after I hug her that she starts shivering.

———

The lack of sleep is catching up with me. I drink cup after cup of coffee, but it does nothing to stop my drooping eyelids. I try to stay on my feet and be productive. I check on Mattie every half hour. At lunchtime, I bring her a sandwich and some yogurt. She just leaves the food on her bedside table, untouched.

After forcing myself to nibble on a sandwich of my own, I retreat to the bathroom. I am fading. I fill a glass with water and use it to wash down some caffeine pills, but I am not quick enough. Too late, I realize I'm holding the Scooby-Doo glass that Officer Teahen used the day he visited our house.

Too late, I realize he must have imprinted on the glass.

Too late, I realize I'm going to slide.

I fall to the bathroom floor in a heap.

———

Officer Teahen is sweating. His shirt is damp with moisture. When he was at our house that day, he seemed so calm and collected as he questioned Mattie. But now, I realize his heart is pounding. He does a great job of hiding his feelings.

He's in a bare room with cement walls, furnished with only a table and two folding chairs. Hanging from the ceiling, a fluorescent light illuminates every corner. A mirror stretches almost the entire length of one wall, and I've seen enough cop shows to know this is a two-way mirror. Seated at the table, looking extremely ill, is Mr. Golden.

Officer Teahen takes out the same little notepad he used when he questioned Mattie and retrieves a pencil from his pocket. "Tell me again, *why* were you at the high school last night?" He turns around to face Mr. Golden.

"I wasn't feeling well, so I was preparing my lesson plans for the substitute teacher." Beads of sweat materialize on Mr. Golden's forehead.

"What time was this?"

"Um, about nine forty-five."

Officer Teahen makes a note of the time. "Tell me what happened then. Don't leave anything out."

Mr. Golden takes a deep breath. "Well, I waved to Eddie—the night custodian—and went to my classroom. I wrote my lesson plans on the board and set out some work sheets on my desk. Then I left."

"How long did this take?" Officer Teahen taps his pencil against the notepad thoughtfully.

"Fifteen minutes. Maybe twenty."

"And that's when you heard the shot?"

Mr. Golden squeezes his eyes shut. "Yes. About ten fifteen."

"And what did you do then?"

Mr. Golden opens his eyes. "I went out to the football field, where I heard the shot. And I found—I called 911 right away."

Officer Teahen takes a minute to ask the next question. I get the sense he's struggling with how to phrase it. Finally, he asks, "Mr. Golden, what was your relationship with Amber Prescott?"

Mr. Golden looks dazed. "She was in my sixth-period class."

"Nothing beyond that? You never spoke with her outside of school?"

"No." Mr. Golden sounds agitated.

"What about Sophie Jacobs? What was your relationship with her?"

"She was in my eighth period."

"Some students have stated that they saw you driving her in your vehicle. Is that true?"

Mr. Golden shrugs nervously. "I gave her a ride home sometimes."

"That was it?"

Mr. Golden pauses, and Officer Teahen rushes on. "Mr. Golden, were you aware that Sophie Jacobs was pregnant?"

Mr. Golden bows his head. After a long, long moment, he whispers, "Yes."

———

Mattie's scream brings me back. The noise is multilayered, peel upon peel of shock and terror. I am crumpled on the bathroom floor.

"Mattie, stop. It's okay. I'm okay." I crawl toward her and pull myself to my feet. As she nestles her head into the crook of my neck, her screams subside.

I hear the front door open.

"Girls?" my father calls. Mattie breaks away from me and races toward the sound of his voice. I follow her down the stairs and watch them embrace. He squeezes her tight, and it makes me wish I could feel the warmth of him.

"Are you girls okay?" It's a dumb question. He turns a little pink.

The officer's conversation with Mr. Golden hangs somewhere in the back of my head. I need to get away, go someplace to sort out my thoughts.

"I'm going out," I announce, grabbing my jacket from the coatrack.

"Where are you going?" my father demands, grabbing my wrist, sounding panicked. I know he's afraid to be alone with Mattie and her grief, but I need a break. I shake him off.

"Out. I'll be back in a few hours."

With that, I slip out the door.

———

I walk quickly to keep warm. It seems the temperature is dipping lower every day now. Before long, the dead leaves will be covered with snow. Pure, white snow. That thought cheers me a little.

In my head, I replay the scene at the police station. It seems clear that Officer Teahen believes Golden is involved with the girls' deaths somehow. He seemed to be insinuating that the teacher was having an inappropriate relationship with Sophie or Amber or both of them. If you'd asked me a few weeks ago whether Golden was capable of such a thing, I'd have said hell no. He was a cool teacher. Everyone liked him. But I guess appearances can be deceiving.

I turn onto the next street, Arbor. At the very end is a light-blue house with a picket fence. Until recently, a slanted For Sale sign had been stuck in the front yard. This is the house Zane was talking about. This is where he lives.

Without thinking, I climb the porch and gently rap on the door with my knuckles. A moment passes, and I hear voices somewhere in the house. I hear someone tromping on the stairs.

Zane flings open the door and looks at me in surprise. "Vee. What are you doing here? Is everything okay?"

"Yes. No. I'm just . . . I need a jelly doughnut."

Zane's eyebrows knit together. "I don't have any left. I'm sorry." His earnestness makes me smile, in spite of myself.

"Oh, no. Metaphorical jelly doughnuts, you know? I need to talk."

"Ah," he says. "Metaphorical jelly doughnuts I can do. You want to sit down?" He motions toward a couple of rocking chairs. I ease into one and survey the street. The neighborhood I've lived in my whole life seems different somehow, from this angle.

"What's up?"

A sob bubbles up in my throat. I clamp my hands over my mouth, a little embarrassed at the sound. I've only known this boy for a few days. I'm really starting to like him. Do I really want to bawl like a baby in front of him?

Zane sits in the chair next to me and pries away one of my hands. He holds it in his own, soft and hard at the same time. He slides his finger back and forth over the skin between my thumb and pointer finger. It makes me shiver.

"Someone else died," I say. "Another of my sister's friends."

He leans forward, concerned. I tell him about my father's phone call and how I spent the whole day watching over Mattie.

I tell him I'm scared. So scared.

I'm scared my sister won't make it through this alive.

Through it all, he keeps rubbing my hand, and it's his touch that gives me the courage to keep going. When I finish, we just sit there. Across the street, a girl in a purple cape chases a small, yapping dog. Oh, what I wouldn't give to be that girl.

I fold myself into the space between his arm and his body. I let myself melt into him, and I can feel him pressing back into me.

"Zane?"

"Yeah?"

"You told me about a sister. What happened?"

He draws a breath, then lets it out slowly. "She died in the hospital shortly after she was born. I don't know what exactly was wrong with her. My mom doesn't like to talk about it."

His eyes dim as he speaks. I think about all the pain he's gone through in his life—his father's suicide, his sister's death. I wonder if some of us are just destined to know tragedy personally. We are alike that way.

"That must have been so hard."

"Like I said, I don't remember much about her. I worry about my mom, though. Ever since we've been back, it's like the past has started to haunt her. She walks around in a sort of haze. I try to get her to go out, do things, meet people. But she won't. She's . . . fixated."

His worry about his mother touches me. I wrap my arms around him, tight. He nuzzles his nose into the hollow of my neck, and then follows with his lips.

As he kisses me, I feel like the lies and death and evil that surround me slowly melt away, and I am new again.

CHAPTER NINETEEN

I look in on Mattie before I leave for school. She doesn't stir. She sleeps the dreamless sleep of Ambien, but that's a good thing. Without it, I don't know what she'd dream of. Dying cheerleaders, broken bodies. She's better off blank. For a moment, I pause, wondering if I shouldn't stay home to watch over her, but I figure she'll be safe with my dad.

In the driveway, Zane waits. I buckle my seat belt, though it won't do anything to protect me from the wreck that awaits us at school. The principal has dismissed regular classes for the day and arranged an assembly.

When we arrive at school, we have to park across the street because the football field and most of the parking lot are blocked off with yellow police tape.

A couple of kids from Wise Choices usher everyone into the gym. They wear T-shirts that say *feeling blue? tell someone*. The bleachers are packed with antsy students and a few concerned-looking parents. I stand at the bottom for a moment, eyeing the stands. Rollins is nowhere to be seen. Neither is Scotch, for that matter.

The air buzzes with rumors. Everyone has their own theory about what happened to Amber. Some kids whisper that she was jealous of Sophie's affair with Mr. Golden. Others say she killed herself out of guilt for pushing Sophie to the edge. Everyone knows how she sent that naked picture of Sophie to the entire football team.

I want to scream my suspicions out loud. *Sophie didn't kill herself. Amber didn't kill herself. There is a murderer among us, and everyone better watch out.* Instead, I concentrate on putting one foot in front of the other as Zane and I climb the bleachers. We find seats in the back, overlooking the entire student body and the nervous, shuffling teachers.

Zane squeezes my hand. "Everything is going to be okay." Even though I'm sure he's wrong, I appreciate the effort.

Three gigantic screens are set up on the gym floor. The middle one is parallel with the bleachers, and the other two are angled inward. Suddenly, the lights go out, and a projector begins flashing images and words onto the screens to the beat of a loud rock song. The pictures are of attractive, yet depressed, teenagers. A redhead fights with her friends. A guy in a baseball cap mopes on the steps in front of his school, his head in his hands. A beautiful blonde stands in front of a mirror, contemplating a bottle of pills.

Words like *sadness*, *loneliness*, and *depression* are interspersed with the pictures. The show goes on for about five minutes, and then one last slide pops up, stretching across all three screens. It's the number for a suicide hotline.

"I think I'm going to be sick," I mutter.

It's gotten so hot. I can't breathe. I Need. To. Get. Out. Of. Here.

Releasing Zane's hand, I rise to go. He stands, as if to come with me, but I push him away. I just want to be alone. I just need the space to breathe. Somehow, I manage to pick my way down the bleachers and slip out of the gym.

The air in the hallway is much cooler. I lean against a trophy case filled with polished gold footballs and basketballs and squeeze my eyes shut, trying to figure out what bothered me so much about the assembly—beyond the obvious fact that it was arranged under completely false assumptions.

I think, though, that I still would have been sickened, even if Sophie and Amber really had committed suicide. There was something so commercial about it, something contrived. It was like the slide show was designed by MTV. I'm on *True Life: Someone Is Killing All the Cheerleaders and Making It Look Like Suicide.*

When the vomity feeling passes, I wander away from the display case, down the hall, toward the girls' bathroom. I round a corner and stop dead in my tracks.

Halfway down the hall, Scotch is shuffling some papers inside a locker.

I take a step backward, out of sight. What would Scotch be doing in the freshman hallway? After a few seconds, I hear a locker door slam. I tense up when I hear his footsteps, but they get softer and softer. He's going the other way.

Cautiously, I poke my head out to see if he's gone. I

glimpse the back of his jacket as he turns a corner and heads toward the student exit. Something black is crumpled on the floor about halfway down the hallway.

I count to ten, in case Scotch realizes he dropped something and comes back for it. When he doesn't, I come out from my hiding spot and make my way toward the black thing. It's a leather glove.

A thought flashes through my mind: *Maybe I can use this.*

I don't know why I didn't think of it before. I've always thought of my sliding as a disability, something that happened *to* me without my consent. But what if I could somehow force myself to slide while holding that glove?

The idea of entering Scotch's head chills me. Every time I see him, I feel physically ill. I was barely able to handle my encounter with him when I slid into Amber. Would I really be capable of purposefully sliding into him?

I picture my sister—at home, in bed, in an Ambien coma. Helpless. If I don't do something to figure out who the killer is, she could very well be next.

I make my decision. I swoop down, pick up the glove, and stuff it into my pocket. Once it's there, I get a little paranoid that Scotch will realize he dropped his glove and come back, so I backtrack toward the gym.

All the classrooms are dark and empty, except for one—Mr. Golden's room. When I passed by it before, I hadn't noticed the light on, but now I realize someone is inside. I approach it cautiously and stand just outside the door, peeking in. Principal Nast is standing with his back to me, and Mr. Golden is sitting at his desk, looking down at his folded hands. I step back slightly so that he won't see me if he looks up.

Mr. Nast speaks first, sounding kind of embarrassed. "Joe, is it true that you knew about Sophie Jacobs's pregnancy?"

A pause.

"Yes. She came in on Friday to talk to me about the situation."

Nast clears his throat. "Can you tell me who the father is?"

"I'm sorry, Steve, but I just don't feel comfortable giving you that information. The girl is dead. Shouldn't she have some privacy?"

"Here's the thing. I've been getting some complaints. All these rumors are making parents nervous about you teaching their kids. Any information you gave me at this point would help me to clear your name. Otherwise, I'm going to need you to take a leave of absence until this thing blows over."

Another pause.

"Joe, I'm trying to help you here."

Mr. Golden says nothing.

Mr. Nast makes a frustrated sound and exits the room. As he passes by me, I turn to a random locker and spin the lock. He glares at me before heading toward the gym. When he's gone, I peer into Mr. Golden's room. He hasn't moved. He's just sitting there, staring at his hands.

The new, proactive me whispers that I should try to get some information from him. Even if he is the killer, there's not much he can do to me here at school. Maybe I can even sneak something with his imprint on it, something that will help me check up on him later.

"Mr. Golden?" I take a step inside. He raises his head, looking confused at the sound of his own name. "Hey . . . uh, I had some questions about the reading assignment. Do you have a minute?"

He stares at me like I'm from another planet.

"Mr. Golden? Are you okay?"

He heaves an enormous sigh. "I can't believe this is my life." He seems to be talking to himself more than to me. He goes to the closet, pulls out a box, and returns to his desk. He starts throwing random things inside—a half-empty bag of cough drops, a stuffed Homer Simpson doll, some *Newsweek* magazines.

"People have been talking. They think I had something to do with the deaths." He forms his syllables in a simple monotone—no inflection whatsoever. He doesn't sound angry or upset or anything. Just numb.

"Why would they think that?" I ask carefully.

"Because people want someone to blame," Mr. Golden replies bitterly. "Sophie came to me for help. I go to her church, and I know her family. When she got pregnant, she asked me for advice. I guess someone saw us together and got the wrong idea."

I think carefully about his words. Would a teacher drive a student around, even if they were a friend of the family? Even if they did go to church together? It still seems suspicious.

"Now that Amber's dead, people are making up all kinds of stories. I tell you, people just want to believe the worst." He mutters something about a "goddamn witch hunt" and then goes back to packing up his things.

"So what are you going to do?" I ask, looking around his room for something that would fit in my pocket.

"What *can* I do? I'm going to go home."

I hear voices in the hallway. The assembly must be over.

"I should leave," I say.

"You probably should," Mr. Golden says, turning back to his desk.

That's when I see it—sitting right there, in plain sight. It was there all the time. Why didn't I notice it before?

The desk calendar.

It looks so harmless—just a plain desk calendar that you'd pick up at any office supply store. White pages, the month and date in a thick, black font. Just like the page that was stuck to my front door the day Sophie died.

I feel like I can't breathe. My heart is hammering underneath my shirt. Somehow, I force myself to turn around naturally and head for the door. I look back once, to make sure Mr. Golden is still focused on packing, and then I dart my hand out and grab a tiny figurine from the bookshelf next to the door.

And then I'm gone.

———

I feel my phone vibrate in my pocket as I tread my way through the sea of students.

"Hello?"

It's my father. "Hey, Vee—could you do me a favor and

pick up Mattie's books? I have a feeling she'll be missing at least a few more days. It'd be nice if she could make up some schoolwork at home."

"Uh, sure," I say, and then hang up. When I put my phone away, I pull the stolen figurine out of my pocket. It's a tiny bronze statue of Sigmund Freud. It seems like the sort of thing Mr. Golden would cherish. Sticking it back in my pocket, I hope he's left some sort of emotional charge on the object. I really don't want to return to his room to try to get something else.

Students rush past me, heading for the exit. They chat excitedly, thrilled to get an early start on the weekend. I fight my way toward my sister's locker. A well-placed punch causes it to pop right open.

I gasp.

Everything in her locker has been tossed to the floor— her textbooks, her gym clothes, the pictures of her and Sophie and Amber that had been taped to the inside of the door. All of it is jumbled at the bottom of her locker in a mess.

Kneeling, I pick up a piece of a photograph that's been ripped to pieces. Half of my sister's face, painted to look like a cat, smiles. It's the picture from the state fair last summer.

I try to drop the picture, but it clings to my fingers. It's covered with a sticky, red substance. When I realize what it is, my stomach drops, and I cover my mouth, afraid I'm going to vomit.

The bottom of Mattie's locker is covered in blood.

I open my mouth and scream.

"What's wrong? Vee?" Strong hands grasp my shoulders. I turn around, see that it's Zane, and bury my head against his chest.

———

We're sitting in Zane's car, waiting for the parking lot to clear out. He traces circles on my back with his fingertip as I wait for my dad to pick up the phone.

"Pick up, pick up, pick up."

"Hello?"

"Dad," I say. "Um, I tried to get Mattie's books, but I couldn't remember her combination. Could you ask her for me?" I don't want to tell my father the bottom of Mattie's locker was coated with red paint. I need to figure out what it means first. I just need him to tell me that Mattie's okay.

I listen to him shuffle around, praying that he'll find Mattie safe in her bed. I hear muffled voices, and I let out a sigh of relief. If the mess in Mattie's locker was meant to be a warning, the killer hasn't struck yet.

"She says nineteen, thirty-four, eighty-six," my dad says. "Thanks for doing this."

"No problem," I say, looking at the pile of books stashed by my feet. I tried to clean them off the best I could, but they're still pretty gross. I'll have to figure out how to explain that later, I guess. "I'll be home soon."

I hang up and sit motionless, staring at my phone.

"When is this going to end?" I wonder aloud.

"When is what going to end?" Zane asks.

"This insanity. When is it going to end? Sophie's dead.

Amber's dead. And now someone is targeting my sister." It occurs to me that Scotch was in the hall minutes before me. If he wasn't at the assembly, what was he doing?

"Do you really think someone wants to hurt Mattie?" he asks.

"Why else would someone do that to her locker? It's a pretty sick prank to play on someone right after two of their friends die. God. It looked so much like blood," I say, remembering the way Sophie's white sheets had turned all scarlet and clotty, just like the stuff at the bottom of Mattie's locker. My hands haven't stopped shaking.

"I'm so worried about Mattie," I continue. "She's depressed. Her two best friends are gone. What if . . . What if she tries to . . . ?"

Zane puts a finger to my lips. "It'll be okay. We'll stay with her this weekend. Watch movies. Make sure she doesn't even leave the house."

He's right, I think. *I'll keep her safe by getting to the bottom of all this. I'll figure out how to make myself slide and find out who the killer is. And, somehow, I will make them pay.*

"Vee?" Zane says.

"Yes?" I reply, my mind somewhere else—on sliding and killers and blood. But when he leans in and kisses me, he has my full attention.

He whispers, "I think I'm falling for you."

For some reason, I can't make my mouth work; I can't voice the words that are carved into my heart. Instead of speaking, I wrap my arms around him and hold tight.

CHAPTER TWENTY

Sitting on my bed, I clamp my hand over my mouth and stifle a yawn. I haven't had any caffeine in approximately nine hours—since before I left for school. Bad things happen to me when I don't get my caffeine. Headache, major grouchiness, nausea.

It'll all be worth it if I can find out what happened to Sophie and Amber before the killer strikes again, I think as I rub my temples.

When my eyelids feel like lead weights, I decide it is time. I hold Scotch's glove in my bare hands. I rub the material, the coarseness making my skin crawl.

I wait.

Nothing happens.

I wait some more.

Nothing.

This isn't as easy as I thought it would be, I think, slapping the glove against my thigh. I suppose it's possible Scotch never imprinted on the glove. He doesn't seem like the most emotional person in the world.

What will I do if it doesn't work? I picture myself sneaking into Scotch's house late at night and grabbing something I know he cares about. Something like a football or a girlie magazine. I'm just fooling myself, though. It would be stupid to break into a possible killer's house. This *has* to work.

Beside me, my phone rings. Rollins again. He's been calling all afternoon. Each time, I let it go to voicemail. At first, he left messages for me to call him back. Now he just hangs up when I don't answer.

It's not that I don't want to talk to him. I do. I want him to explain exactly what he was doing with Amber on that field moments before her death. The thing is, I can't ask him that question. I can't explain how I know he was there. And until I know for sure who killed Sophie, I can't risk letting him get close to me—and more importantly, to Mattie.

The phone goes silent.

Good.

I return to my task. Rubbing the glove against my cheek, I inhale the scent of Scotch. Of sweat, of orange shampoo. Of that night so long ago. My stomach turns over.

The seconds slip by. Soon I start to feel sleepy.

The room goes dark, and I lose my grip on the present. I slide.

———

A dark room materializes around me, lit only by a football game on the television. Faux wood paneling stretches from one wall to the next. There are several framed posters featuring football players I don't recognize. I'm lounging in a leather chair, a can of something cold in my hand. Scotch lifts the drink and takes a sip. Expecting something sweet, I'm surprised at the bitter taste that fills my mouth.

Beer.

What is Scotch doing drinking beer in the den in the middle of the afternoon?

He opens his mouth, and a deep voice—much deeper than Scotch's—calls out, "Tricia? Trish! I thought I told you to make me a damn sandwich."

A petite woman enters my line of vision, holding another beer in one hand and a plate in the other.

"Sorry, Hank. I was just finishing up some laundry."

Hank.

Not Scotch.

I've slid into his father.

Damn.

———

I wake up on my bed, pillow cushioning my head.

Someone thumps on my door and then opens it without waiting for an answer.

"Vee?" My father looks in. "Did you bring home Mattie's books?"

"Um, yeah," I say, sitting up. I point to a pile of books sitting on my mother's rocking chair. Each of them has a trace of red paint left, even though I tried to clean them off. "Unfortunately, I set them down in the hall while I went to the bathroom, and the custodian was walking by with a can of paint. And he tripped . . ."

I look at my father's face to gauge whether he's buying any of this at all. He drifts into the room, nodding distractedly. I don't think he's even paying attention.

"So that assembly you went to today—was it helpful? They talked to you about the warning signs of suicide, right?" My father ruffles his hands through his hair.

"Right," I say, even though I didn't sit through the whole thing.

He sits down heavily on my bed. "Did Sophie or Amber exhibit any of those signs?"

His question catches me off guard. I try to remember the warning signs. I know the counselors told us all about them when we were in middle school. The only one I recall is giving away personal belongings. I shiver when I remember Sophie giving me the bracelet to give to Mattie. But that was a gift . . . It doesn't count, does it?

"I don't know. They weren't exactly *my* friends."

"I think I'm going to call Dr. Moran. Mattie should have someone to talk to. Someone who knows about these things."

Hearing the name of my old psychiatrist irritates me. She's the cold, unsympathetic woman my father sent me to when he thought I was lying about sliding. The one who accused me of making up stories for attention. I know Mattie probably needs professional help, but I hate the thought of sending her to that robot.

"Whatever," I mutter, but my father has already risen and is crossing to the door.

For once, I wish he'd realize that what Mattie needs is *him*.

———

After dinner, I have an idea. A breakthrough.

I fling open my closet door and stand there for a moment, my heart pounding. Then I push my clothes aside until I come to the one garment I know Scotch had his hands on—the purple dress I wore to homecoming.

My hands shaking, I carry the dress over to my bed and carefully spread it out. I smooth my hands over it. The fabric sparkles as it moves. As I stare at the dress, I'm filled with certainty that this will work. The dress will put me in Scotch's head. I've been going about it all wrong. Clearly, Scotch never imprinted on the glove. But this dress—I know he felt something strong when he touched this dress.

I kneel at the side of my bed and rest my hands lightly on the material. And, just as I knew it would, the room fades away.

———

Tombstones. Everywhere.

Scotch is in the cemetery. The sun has sunk low in the sky. It also seems several degrees colder than it did when I was outside, but then I realize it must be because Scotch only has one glove. He raises his bare hand to his mouth and blows into it, the hot air warming it only slightly.

A huge, gnarled tree looms over us. When Scotch passes it, I see a woman in a red coat stooped in front of a tiny gravestone, clutching a fistful of daisies. She kneels down and brushes away some leaves, and I'm able to read the inscription.

allison morrow
october 17, 1998–october 19, 1998

Sadness squeezes my heart. The baby died after only two days of life. If the child had lived, she'd be in my sister's grade.

The woman at the grave turns toward Scotch and brushes her white hair out of her face. Her eyes are black as coal and filled with sadness, and I wonder what losing a child that young does to you. I'm reminded of the passage on black holes in my astronomy book, how they suck everything in until no light remains. That's what seeing your kid die would feel like.

Scotch must feel the pull of her misery, too, but he looks away and continues walking. We pass by the nine-foot statue of an angel that used to be bronze. Years of harsh weather have turned it black. Rumor has it, if you kiss the angel, you will drop dead within one year.

Scotch keeps going until he comes to a delicate, white, brand-new tombstone.

sophie jacobs

Scotch just stands there, staring at the piece of stone that marks the grave of a girl who might have carried his child. Again, I wish I could know his thoughts. Why would he come here? To gloat that he got away with murder? To make amends? To mourn?

He reaches out his naked hand and traces Sophie's name with his fingers. "I wish it could have been different, Soph. I really do." He retrieves his hand and pushes it into his pocket. "I guess God just really wanted me to go on and use that football scholarship."

A terrible rage rises within me. The fury is energy, begging to be used. Gathering all my strength, I form Scotch's hand into a fist and slam it into his balls. The pain is beyond belief, but I know it's so much worse for him.

He screams, and it's the last thing I hear as I'm pulled away from his body.

CHAPTER TWENTY-ONE

I toss and turn, trying to turn my mind off, trying to will myself to fall asleep, but I'm not tired at all. Actually, I've never felt so alive, so energized. When I guided Scotch's muscles, it was like I was inside him, only not. It was like a video game, like I was pushing buttons with my mind, and he did what I told him. It was invigorating.

For so long, I've been out of control, popping in and out of people's heads, prisoner to their choices and actions. Now there is a sliver of light, of hope, that I can *choose*.

If I slide into a teacher making out with a bus driver during school hours, I can choose to push him and his disgusting mustache away.

If I slide into Scotch when he's putting his hands all over some clueless cheerleader, I can *choose* to neuter him. Oh, and don't think I won't.

If I slide into someone standing in a dark room and there's the smell of blood and I see a body on the bed, I can . . .

I can . . .

I can't do anything about that.

I can't do anything about Sophie.

And I can't do anything about Amber, either.

But *now*. Now that I have some control, maybe I can keep any more girls from dying. Maybe I can protect my sister.

I jump onto my bed and start doing ninja kicks and punching the air. I am Buffy, ready to kick some bad-guy ass. Laughter erupts from my throat, and I flop down onto my bed and stare at the planet and star stickers on my ceiling.

This feeling of being in charge of my own life is intoxicating. I feel drunk or high or something. I want to use my new power, want to experiment.

I slip out of my bedroom and tiptoe down the hall. I peer down the stairs and see light coming from my father's office. He's probably busy with his online forum, comforting cancer survivors, saying just the right things to them because he doesn't have to sit across from them at dinner.

I continue down the hall, to his bedroom. The door is slightly ajar. I push it the rest of the way open and look around. His room is perfectly neat. The bed is made, and—unlike my room—there are no clothes on the floor. There's nothing on top of the chest of drawers except an old picture of my mother.

My father keeps his and my mother's wedding rings in a velvet box in the top right drawer of the bureau. For years after her death, he kept wearing his ring, until an old lady on the cancer survivors' forum told him he should take it off. For once, he took someone else's advice instead of dishing it out. When I noticed he wasn't wearing it anymore, I asked him about it. He assured me he was keeping it safe, but it was painful to keep looking down at his hand and missing Mom all day long. Sometimes I go and open the drawer and open the box—not to touch the rings, but just to look at them. This time, I carefully pull my father's ring out of the box.

I've slid into my father before—accidentally, when I tried on his watch or flipped through an old photo album. Once I slid into him in the middle of an operation, and that pretty much scarred me for life. But since I know he's downstairs right now, messing around on the computer, I figure he's the perfect target for my little test.

Back in my room, I hop onto my bed and cup the ring in my palm.

I sit there for a long time, waiting for something— anything—to happen. The minutes pass by slowly. After a while, I start to get paranoid that my father will come upstairs and look in his drawer. There's no reason for him to, but I guess that's the nature of paranoia.

I slip the ring onto my finger and lie back on my pillow. My headache from earlier returns, and it seems like the caffeine pills in my backpack are actually calling out to me, begging me to swallow a few of them. Ignoring the pain, I close my eyes.

And feel myself go.

———

I find myself in my father's office, sitting before his computer. He's reading an email from some lady who lost her son to cancer last year. For a moment he stares at the screen, probably thinking of how to phrase his response. Then he hits Reply and types a few sentences expressing his condolences and recommending a book that will help her manage her grief.

After sending that email, he minimizes the page with the cancer survivor forum and pulls up an online medical journal. He clicks through a couple of articles, reading about recent surgeries. It's pretty boring. I wonder if I should make him pick his nose or something, just to see if I can do it.

I concentrate all my energy into his right pointer finger. *Come on, finger,* I think. *Pick Dad's nose.* But the finger just keeps floating around the trackpad on my dad's computer, navigating him through article after boring article.

Frustrated, I try to figure out why I can't control my father like I controlled Scotch in the cemetery. The only thing I can come up with is the rage I felt when Scotch said he thought Sophie's death was for the best. Maybe adrenaline has something to do with it.

The phone rings, and my dad jumps a little. He brings the phone to his ear and says hello, but all I hear is heavy breathing.

"Hello? Hello?" my father repeats, annoyance edging his voice. No one replies. "Goddamn it, this is the last straw. If you call here again, I'm going to call the police." Whoever is on the other end hangs up the phone.

I wonder who was on the other end. I'm filled with apprehension as I remember the phone call I overheard the other day when he was telling someone it was over. Could my father have a stalker?

He sits quietly for a second before hanging up, staring at the wedding picture of my mother. He takes it in his hands.

I expect him to caress my mother's image or kiss it or something, but instead he flips it over and unhooks the back. To my surprise, he reveals a tiny silver key taped to the underside of the photograph. Carefully, he unpeels the tape and takes the key into his hand. Then he reassembles the frame and returns the picture to his desk.

I watch in astonishment as he takes the little key and guides it into the lock on the bottom drawer of the desk.

My parents bought the desk from a flea market ages ago. When we were little, my sister and I used it to play teacher. We tried to pull the drawer open, but it never budged. Dad said the previous owner of the desk had lost the key, but it was so beautiful he just had to have it anyway.

He lied.

He pulls the drawer open and shoves his hand inside, searching roughly for something. Finally he pulls out a manila folder. Across the front, written in my father's messy handwriting, is the name Allison. He flips it open, revealing a thick sheaf of papers. On the very top is a photograph of a gorgeous woman with white-blond hair.

The realization is sudden—I have seen that woman before. In the cemetery, when I slid into Scotch. She was standing before a tombstone. A tombstone marked "*Allison Morrow*". Trying to piece it all together, I wonder who exactly that woman was. And who the hell is Allison?

My father's hands shake as he puts the folder back in the drawer, minus the picture of the white-haired woman. He stares at the picture for a moment longer, before crinkling it up in his fist. He tosses the picture into the wastebasket beneath his desk.

"Leave. Me. Alone," he whispers.

He then locks the drawer back up and puts the key back in its hiding place, behind my mother's picture.

Slowly, I feel myself being pulled away, back into my own body.

———

I wait half an hour after I hear my father go into his room and then open my door silently. Down the hall, my father's room is quiet, no light peeking beneath the door. I pray that he's asleep. I tiptoe down the stairs, the cold wood freezing my bare feet.

My father's office is dark, lit only by the moonlight coming through the window. It really is a dreary place, now that I think about it. When my mother was alive, she decorated every room to her taste, bringing in paintings and floral prints and pretty mirrors. But my dad never let her touch this room. He doesn't even let Vanessa clean in here. There's a layer of sludge on the windows. This room is full of his things, his dusty secrets.

I dash across the room and snatch up the picture of my mother. Removing the back of the frame, I find the key just where my father left it, shining so brightly it seems as though it's daring me to use it.

I stare at it for a moment. What will it lead me to? I don't know. I'm not sure I'm ready to know, but I don't know if I'll ever really be ready, so I carefully peel away the tape and weigh the key in the palm of my hand. So light, yet so heavy at the same time.

Kneeling down, I position the key by the lock. For a split second, I chicken out. This is my dad, the guy who cooks us chocolate-chip pancakes every Sunday morning. He has to have a good reason for keeping whatever it is locked up in there.

Doesn't he?

My eyes flicker involuntarily to the trash can, willing the picture of the white-haired woman to be gone. Maybe it was all in my head. All my imagination. But there it still is.

I'm tired of secrets.

I'm ready for truth.

I force the key into the lock and twist until I hear a little click release somewhere inside the wooden desk. I set the key on top of the desk and pull open the drawer. The manila folder sits on top of a bunch of old medical journals. I snatch the folder up and rifle through the papers within. They're some kind of records.

I pull out a paper and examine it.

Name: Allison Annette Morrow

Allison. The name from the tombstone. The girl who died after only a couple of days. Why would my father be keeping her medical records?

I continue reading. There's a bunch of gibberish I don't

understand. She was born prematurely with an anorectal malformation and required immediate surgery. I flip a page. Numbers. Jargon.

I turn to the last page in the folder.

```
Date of death: October 19, 1998
```

October 19. Allison Annette Morrow died in surgery just over fourteen years ago under my father's knife. And he keeps her medical records in a drawer, never to forget. I feel sick.

Why her?

I know he's lost babies before.

Why hold on to this one failure?

My hands shaking, I replace the folder on top of the magazines. I lock the drawer and return the key to its hiding place.

It takes me a long, long time to fall asleep.

CHAPTER TWENTY-TWO

Today is Mattie's birthday, and I haven't gotten her a thing. I only remember when I see the special breakfast casserole on the kitchen table—the one my father reserves for birthdays or other special occasions. Eggs and bacon and cheese and potatoes. And butter. Lots and lots of butter. Normally, I live for this sort of thing, but these words keep sliding around my head: *anorectal malformation*. I Googled the term last night, but knowing the medical details didn't help much. I want to know exactly what happened on October 19, 1998 and why my father has held on to it for so long. What's so special about this Allison? And what's his connection with the white-haired woman I saw in the cemetery? *Is* there any connection? Or am I just going crazy?

I don't know how to broach this topic. Plus, Mattie has actually brushed her hair and is sitting at the table, looking hungry, so I don't want to do anything to mess that up.

"So, what do you want to do for your big day, birthday girl?" My dad heaps a pile of casserole onto a plate and passes it to Mattie. The forced cheeriness in his voice seems to highlight how crappy this day actually is.

Mattie shrugs and then pushes a fork into the big melty cheesy mess in front of her. "I don't know. Just hang out around here? I don't really feel like going out."

"That sounds great. Maybe we could rent *Mulan* tonight? Order pizza for dinner? Would you like that?"

"Dad, I haven't liked *Mulan* since the second grade," Mattie replies. There's no resentment in her voice, like there would have been had I said it. It's just a simple fact.

"Well, how about the first season of *Rumor Girl*? I've heard great things." My father's face is so earnest; it's almost painful to look at.

"Um, you mean *Gossip Girl*? Sure. Yeah, okay." My sister takes another glob of casserole into her mouth.

Could my father really be hiding some deep, dark secret? This man who wants to watch *Gossip Girl* with his teenage daughters? Is this just a facade so we won't suspect what he's *really* up to?

"I'm not feeling well," I say. "I'm going to go lie down."

Passing by my sister, I squeeze her shoulder. "Happy birthday, Matt."

She turns her head my way and gives me the most heart-breaking smile. "Thanks."

Guilt follows me up the stairs and into my room. I really should give her something to acknowledge her birthday— but what?

I scan my belongings, wondering if there's anything I have that she could possibly want. My closet door is ajar, and the box of my mother's CDs is sticking out slightly.

With a tug, I heave the box into the middle of the room.

One by one, I pull the CDs out and spread them all over the floor. Pearl Jam. The Smashing Pumpkins. Veruca Salt. Nirvana. Liz Phair. Ani DiFranco. This is what I have left of my mother, the music she lived her life by.

This is what I have to give to my sister, who was so little when my mother died, who can no longer remember that my mother's hair always smelled like violets or how the corners of her eyes crinkled when she smiled or how she cackled like a witch when she found something really hilarious.

I pick up the Smashing Pumpkins CD and hold it to my cheek. The plastic is cold from sitting in my drafty closet for so long. Then I put it back in the box. I go through this process with each CD, holding it close for just one more moment and then putting it away.

When I've loaded the CDs all back into the box, I push the flaps closed and carry it to my sister's room. She hasn't returned from breakfast yet, so I place the box on her unmade bed and leave the room.

I've attached a pink Post-it note. It says:

THIS IS WHO SHE WAS.
LOVE, V

CHAPTER TWENTY-THREE

I lean back against my pillow, holding the tiny Sigmund Freud and wondering if it is personal enough to provide me with a link to Mr. Golden. It seems like the sort of thing someone would give you for a present. Maybe a family member? A former student? A girlfriend? I rub my thumb over the figure, thinking about what he might have witnessed in Mr. Golden's room.

Yawning, I turn the little man over. That's when I notice the markings on the bottom. It's been engraved. The letters are so tiny; I have to squint to make out the message.

YOU HYPNOTIZE ME. N.P.

Hmmmm. N.P. Who could that be? Well, one thing's clear—it's a personal item, all right. I just hope he was stirred with enough emotion when he received it to leave an imprint.

When my head starts to pound and black floaty things swim before my eyes, I know he was. My room disappears, and I am swallowed by the blackness.

Mr. Golden stands before a white door decorated with an orange-and-brown wreath. He balls his right hand into a fist and raps on the door, then takes a step back to wait for an answer. The door opens, revealing a familiar, grief-stricken face. It is Amber Prescott's father. His hair is mussed, and his eyes are rimmed red.

"Mr. Prescott?" Mr. Golden asks, his voice unsure. "I'm Mr. Golden, Amber's teacher. I called earlier. I have the journal she kept in class. Thought you might want it?" He waves a notebook in the air halfheartedly. "Is this a bad time?"

"Uh, no," Amber's father replies, but his voice seems far away, like he's speaking through a fog. "Come in. You can call me Trent."

Mr. Golden steps into the entryway. I survey the scene in agony. I was here once before, briefly, to pick up Mattie from a sleepover. I remember, at the time, being impressed by the simple, elegant decor of the room, from the perfect eggshell paint color to the black suede couch and love seat. The focal point of the room was a painting of purple irises blowing in the wind.

Now, the beautiful painting is askew. Overturned on the coffee table is a single crystal glass in a puddle of brown liquid. The smell assures me that it's something alcoholic. On the muted television, Seinfeld looks like he's laughing.

"Would you care for a drink?"

"Ah, no. Can't stay long. Is your wife around?"

Amber's father eases into a black leather recliner, his eyes glued to the television set. "Back room. She won't come out. Why don't you take the journal to her? It might give her some comfort, to read Amber's words."

Mr. Golden stands there awkwardly for a second, and I'm sure he's considering just tossing the notebook onto the coffee table and getting the hell out of here. That's what I'd be thinking about, anyway. But he surprises me.

He turns and heads down the long hallway, where he must figure the "back room" is. Both walls are lined with pictures. In one, a little Amber stands next to a horse, proudly holding up her blue ribbon. In another, Amber looks to be about ten and sits with her arm hanging casually over her younger brother's shoulder. In yet another, she is older, grinning in a crisp City High cheerleading outfit. She smiles the kind of smile only popular girls own the right to—kind of like, "The world is mine, and that's how it should be." This is the Amber I knew.

The door to the room at the end of the hall is slightly ajar. Mr. Golden holds out his hand and gently pushes it open. For a moment, all I can see is light flickering from votive candles scattered around the floor. Then I realize Amber's mother is sitting in the middle of them, her arms wrapped around her knees. She rocks back and forth, back and forth.

"Nora?" Mr. Golden says, barely above a whisper. The disparity in the way he addresses Amber's parents strikes me. Why would he call Amber's father *Mr. Prescott* and her mother *Nora*? The intimacy in the way he said her name is unsettling.

She lifts her head for a moment and then, seeing who it is, lowers it again.

"Nora. I'm here for you." Mr. Golden crouches on the floor next to her. "I'm here." The tenderness in his voice is palpable. And then it hits me: Nora.

N.P.

Nora Prescott.

Amber's mother must have given him the figurine.

It's as if she doesn't even hear him. She speaks, but it's like she's continuing a different conversation. Her words are barely recognizable, and that's when I smell the liquor on her breath.

"I remember her first day of high school. She said she didn't want to go back. She hated the way everyone pretended to be someone they weren't. She didn't know who to be."

This doesn't sound like the Amber I knew—the girl who plotted which date for homecoming would win her the most popularity, the girl who actually took a ruler to her skirts to see how short she could possibly go without getting busted for breaking the dress code. The Amber I knew was kind of a bitch.

"She was scared, and I made her go back anyway."

The woman takes a sip from a drink I hadn't realized she was holding, then sends it flying through the room. It crashes against the wall and shatters in a burst of ice cubes and jagged pieces of glass.

"I made her *go*."

"She had to go to school, Nora. You most certainly didn't make her steal Trent's gun and do what she did. You didn't make her do *that*."

Amber's mother turns and looks Mr. Golden in the eyes for the first time since he entered the room. "She knew about us. The day of Sophie's funeral. She came back just in time to see you leaving. And the next day she shot herself with Trent's gun. Because of us."

My god. The thought that Amber had actually committed suicide never occurred to me. I was sure someone else pulled the trigger, the same someone who dragged the knife across Sophie's wrists. But if Amber stole her father's gun, doesn't that mean she killed herself?

"Now, now, Nora. Are you sure she saw me leave? Maybe she was just overcome with sadness. I mean, her best friend had just committed suicide. She was coming home from the funeral." Mr. Golden glances toward the doorway and then reaches over to push Mrs. Prescott's hair out of her face. He sounds calm, reassuring.

What if Amber did come home after Sophie's funeral and ran into Mr. Golden leaving her house? Did she confront him? Did she threaten to tell her father? And if Mr. Golden had access to Mr. Prescott's wife, could he have had access to Mr. Prescott's gun?

Mr. Golden reaches for Mrs. Prescott's hand. She pushes it away and starts mumbling again. He sighs and gets up, leaving the notebook on the floor.

"I'm sorry, Nora," he says, and then leaves the room without another word.

CHAPTER TWENTY-FOUR

L uckily, when I return, I find my body flopped safely on my bed. I sit up and wipe a bit of drool off my chin. Sliding is not the most glamorous way to get around, that's for sure.

Beside me, my phone rings insistently. Rollins again. My fingers flex, wanting to answer. My gaze falls on the T-shirt he gave me. It lies crumpled on the floor, where I threw it after seeing him with Amber. All I'd have to do is slip it on—I could reassure myself that he had a good reason to meet her that night, that he's not the killer.

I could slide right into his life and find out . . . everything. What he does all those hours he's not at school or work. What he's hiding from me at home. Why he never invites me over. I'm itching to know his secrets, but at the same time I wonder if sliding into him wouldn't be like hacking his email or reading his diary. When I slid into him accidentally, it felt weird, but I knew it wasn't my fault. But if I target him by using that same T-shirt, it would be different. It would be like spying.

I'd be doing it for the right reason—wouldn't I? To clear Rollins's name. If you invade someone's privacy with good intentions, it's not as bad. I close my eyes and remember how we used to be. I miss our silly conversations about who would win in a fight—Chuck Norris or Mr. T. I miss his sardonic smile. I miss the girl I am when I'm around him.

I have to fix things between us, and sliding into him is the only way I know how.

My decision made, I reach down, snag the blue material with my pinky, and pull it onto my lap. Easing back onto my pillows, I hug the fabric to my chin. I'm amazed at how quickly I'm taken away. I'm kind of getting good at this.

———

The smell is acrid, like rotting broccoli and urine. Water stains and cracks work their way down the walls. I'm lying on a mattress with blue flannel sheets, staring up at the ceiling.

A song I know is playing—"Thinking of You" by A Perfect Circle. For a month last year, Rollins was obsessed with this song, playing it on a continuous loop in his car. The drums are intense, beating through my brain.

I'm twirling something in my hands like a baton. Without even looking, I know what it is. A Sharpie. Rollins's sword to tear the world apart. He stops twirling and uses the marker to match the drumbeat on his stomach.

His room is desolate, furnished with only a bed, a small chest of drawers, and a bookshelf packed with old paperbacks. Back when we used to hang out, we'd go to the used bookstore every weekend and buy bags and bags of books. One of his shelves is dedicated to Stephen King novels. I remember him saying his favorite was *The Dead Zone*.

His door swings open, and a guy in a red flannel shirt bursts in. It must be his uncle Ned.

"You didn't do your shit today," the guy says. It's an accusation—of what, I have no idea.

Rollins sits up. "What shit?"

"It's Saturday. Your turn to do the bath."

Rollins swears. "Can't it wait until tomorrow?"

"She's *your* mother." The man points at Rollins.

Sighing, Rollins stands up and pushes past the man. He walks down the hall and calls to a wiry woman in a wheelchair, who's watching cartoons. Her hair is a tangled nest of snarls.

"Time for your bath," Rollins says, his voice terse.

No wonder he's never invited me to his house. From his surly uncle to his incapacitated mother, he has his hands full without worrying about what his friends think of his predicament. I start to worry I made the wrong decision in coming here.

Rollins pushes the woman down the hall and into the bathroom, which looks like it hasn't been cleaned in years. Rollins turns the knob, releasing a gush of water into the tub. He carefully gauges the temperature—not too hot, not too cold.

He helps his mother undress, all the while staring up at the ceiling. She raises her hands, and he pulls off her shirt. She has to lean on him while he lowers her pants and underwear.

I feel that he's turned himself off somehow. He's on autopilot. He helps her into the tub, bearing her weight so she won't slip and fall. He fills a Big Gulp cup and then dumps the water over her head, which makes her clap her hands in glee. When he lathers an old pink washcloth with soap and works it over her shoulders and breasts, I zone out.

Before long, the bath is over and Rollins's mother has been toweled off and returned to her place in front of the television. Rollins lumbers back to his room, his fists clenching and unclenching as he passes his uncle, who's cracking open a beer.

As he enters his room, I catch sight of something I'd missed earlier. Peeking out from underneath his bed—which could more accurately be called a cot—is a jumbled pile of photographs.

He walks closer, and in one of the pictures I'm able to make out the shape of a girl in a red bikini lying on a beach towel. Her black hair flares out around her face, and she wears giant red sunglasses. Sophie. What the—?

Apprehension pulses through me. I have to figure out why he has pictures of Sophie. Before I know it, I'm next to the bed and spreading the photographs across the floor.

A part of me realizes that I'm controlling Rollins, but mostly I'm concerned with the task at hand.

There are pictures of Sophie at school, of her in her cheerleading uniform, even in boxers and a T-shirt with her hair twisted into a french braid. Not only that—there are pictures of Amber Prescott, too.

One photograph in particular catches my eye. I grab it so I can examine it more closely. It's a picture of Amber and Sophie at cheerleading practice. In the background, Samantha Phillips stands on top of the bleachers, a megaphone at her mouth. Rollins has drawn devil horns on top of her flaming red hair and a spiky tail curling by her side. In her hand that's not holding the megaphone, he's fashioned a pitchfork.

Why does Rollins have pictures of dead girls in his room?

I set the photo down and stand up, hoping to find a hint somewhere in the room. A door beckons to me. When I open it, the contents make me sad. Two pairs of jeans, neatly hung on hangers. And his leather jacket, his most prized possession.

There is literally nothing else in the closet.

Just then, I feel myself start to go.

No, I tell myself. I hold on to Rollins with every fiber of my being. But, as easy as it was for me to slide into him, I'm unable to anchor myself in his body. I stagger backward and leave Rollins lying on his bed.

———

Hot water cascades over my shoulders and back, pounding out the tension I've felt since coming out of my latest slide. I tilt my head back and let the water run down my face, thinking about what I saw at Rollins's house.

By sliding into Rollins, I'd been hoping to find the reason for his meeting with Amber on the night of her death. But all I turned up were more questions.

On the bright side, I was able to take control of Rollins. I think it has something to do with my focus. When I controlled Scotch, I was so angry and all I could think about was giving him the beating he so sorely deserved. When I was in Rollins, I was intent on finding out why he had those photographs.

My cell phone, which I set on the edge of the sink in case Zane called while I was showering, begins to ring the generic ring it makes when someone I don't know calls. Squinting, I shut the water off and reach for a towel.

The number flashing on the display looks vaguely familiar, but I can't place it. Iowa City area code, so it's not a telemarketer. I wrap the towel around my torso, tuck the end under my armpit, and pick up the phone.

"Hello?"

"Vee?"

Again, the pang of familiarity strikes, but I can't place the voice that's asking for me.

"Yeah?"

"It's Samantha."

Something like nostalgia hits me, and I wonder if I haven't stepped out of the shower and into last year, when a phone call from Samantha wasn't something unusual. For a minute, I'm speechless, and I just stand there with my mouth open like an idiot.

"Um. Samantha? Why are you calling me? Did you accidentally call the wrong sister? I can go get Mattie for you. It is her birthday, you know . . ."

"Yeah, well, that's sort of why I'm calling."

"Okay . . . so what do you want?"

"I'm organizing a little get-together at my place tonight. But it's a surprise. I asked her if she wanted to come over and watch movies tonight, but she said she wanted to hang out with family . . ." The tone of Samantha's voice makes me roll my eyes, like it's so ridiculous Mattie would ever want to spend time with her family.

"Samantha. Two members of your squad are dead. Isn't it a little . . . insensitive to be throwing a party tonight?"

"That's exactly why we need some fun. I'm guessing Mattie's been just lying around in bed the last couple of days. Am I right? She needs to get out and have some fun. I have her best interests at heart."

"Uh-huh. Well, Mattie can do what she wants. Sorry if that spoils your plans."

Samantha pauses.

"Vee, really. I'm trying to do something nice for Matt. I'm worried about her. With everything that's happened in the past week . . . she needs her friends."

I squelch the snide comment about what kind of a friend I think Samantha is and think of Mattie, shut up in her bedroom like a hermit. It actually would be good for her to get out of the house. Get out of her head. This might not be such a bad idea.

"What do you need me to do?"

"Come to the party. Convince her to go. I'll come and pick you guys up and everything. I know you don't drive . . ."

Her words trail off, and I know our minds are both back in the gym last year, when she watched Scotch drag my lifeless body into the boys' locker room.

"On one condition," I say.

"Anything," she replies, and I swear she's near tears.

"You can't invite Scotch Becker."

"Done."

"Okay. You can pick us up at seven."

My sister's room is dark, with the soft notes of Pearl Jam's "Black" wafting through the air, filling the room with an anguish so thick I feel I could touch it. My sister lies on the floor, wrapped in a pink blanket.

"Mattie?"

"Sssssssh, this is the best part," she says, her eyes closed.

Eddie Vedder sings sadly about pictures washed in black. So many times I've listened to this song, envisioning a shroud over all the pictures of our dead mother. Samantha is right. I have to dig Mattie out of this hole.

"I love this song," I say, tiptoeing to her computer and finding the pause button. "But don't you think you should listen to something a little more upbeat on your birthday?"

When the music stops, my sister sits up indignantly. "Hey."

"Yeah, I know. But I just got a call from Samantha. She wants us to come over tonight to watch movies or some crap. You up for it?"

Mattie narrows her eyes at me. "Since when does Samantha call you?"

I sigh. "We *did* used to be friends. Besides, she's worried about you. Come on. It'll be fun." The word *fun* feels like it's been coated in cyanide. I'm guessing Mattie's too out of it to notice how bad I am at lying, though.

"Ugh. What time?"

"She's going to pick us up at seven. That'll give you a few more hours to roll around in your own filth." I grin.

Mattie sticks out her tongue, and I take that as my dismissal.

CHAPTER TWENTY-FIVE

I stare at myself in the mirror, wondering what I've gotten myself into. A party? At Samantha's house? I haven't been there in over a year.

I get a bad case of déjà vu as I find myself wondering what shade of lip gloss I should wear. Instead, I flop down on my bed, pulling out the astronomy book. The Gin Blossoms serenade me as I read about stellar evolution.

Someone pounds on my door, and then my dad sticks his head in. "Rollins is here. Should I send him up?"

Panicking, I drop my book. I don't feel ready to confront Rollins at all. I need more time to figure out what's going on, what he was doing with those pictures of Sophie and Amber. Then again, maybe this is the perfect time to grill him. I mean, if he *is* the killer, he wouldn't dare murder me in my own bedroom with my dad right down the hall. Right? Except for the fact that the killer murdered Sophie with her parents right down the hall. Shit.

Another knock.

"Come in," I yell, turning down the music.

Rollins pushes my door open, raking discarded T-shirts and music magazines across the floor. His cheeks are flaming, his hair disheveled.

"Hey," he says, a bit uncertainly. "Long time, no see."

I remember ducking down in the kitchen when he stopped by the other day. Did he catch me doing that?

"I know. Sorry. I've just been . . . busy."

The response seems inadequate. What am I supposed to say, though? *I slid into your body when you were meeting a girl who turned up dead the next day? Then I watched you give your mom a bath and found out that you have a stash of dead-girl pictures?*

"With Zane?" Rollins asks. "Yeah, I heard you two have been hanging out a lot." His brown eyes seem to darken a bit, or maybe the room just darkened a little—I can't be sure.

"Well, with Zane, but also—you know, Mattie's been going through a lot. I'm trying to be there for her." I notice he's carrying a pamphlet. Is that what he's been doing the past few days—working on a zine?

"Here," he says, holding out the booklet. "I brought this for you. Hot off the press."

I take the zine and examine it. On the cover, there's a black-and-white photograph of Sophie Jacobs and Amber Prescott in their cheerleading outfits. I recognize the picture from the pile in Rollins's room. He'd gathered pictures of Sophie and Amber for a *zine*? That's what he must have been doing with Amber on the football field that night. I remember Amber passing something to him—it must have been pictures of her and Sophie together.

Across the top, in Sharpie: *Fear and Loathing in High School No. 8: The Sophie Jacobs and Amber Prescott Special Edition*. I flip through the zine. The first section contains memories about the girls from damn near everyone at City High. Next is a list of songs people dedicated to Sophie and Amber. Mattie even got in on the action, dedicating "Stand by Me" to her two dead friends. Why didn't she tell me what Rollins was doing?

Relief bubbles up inside me, and I realize just how much it would have killed me if it turned out that Rollins was the murderer. I grab him by the shoulders and pull him into a bear hug, squeezing him so hard my poor muscles ache.

"Uh, so you like it?"

"This is so beautiful, Rollins. Really." I step back and look him in the face. He seems embarrassed and pulls on his lip ring.

"I wanted to do something. How's Mattie?" He draws a Sharpie out of the pocket of his leather jacket and starts twirling it absentmindedly.

"Not that great. But tonight I'm taking her to this thing at Samantha's house—surprise birthday party. It's going to suck, but at least it'll get Mattie out of the house."

Rollins makes a face. "At *Samantha's*?"

"I know," I say, grimacing. And then I'm overcome with this intense desire to hug Rollins again, the person who knows what happened to me sophomore year, the one who's always been there. How silly I'd been to doubt him.

"I'm sorry for being a bitch to you," I say.

He shrugs. "Tough time for everyone. I get it. Hey, there's something I wanted to talk to you about." He passes the Sharpie from one hand to the other, anxiety radiating off him.

"Sure," I say, and I pull him over to my bed and sit next to him. "What's up?"

He taps the Sharpie on his thigh nervously. "The other night . . ." He pauses, starts over again. "The night that Amber died?"

"Yes?" I urge him to keep going.

"I saw her." His eyes never leave the Sharpie. "I'd asked her for some pictures of Sophie for my zine. She said she'd give them to me, but she wanted me to meet her on the football field. She was acting pretty weird."

I exhale, reassured that my hypothesis about their meeting that night was true. Unfortunately for Amber, she didn't realize she was also providing pictures for her own memorial zine.

"Weird how?" I prompt.

"Well, she told me I should tell Mattie she was sorry and that everything was her fault. And she started crying and said everyone thought she was a whore and that her whole life was a joke. I tried to tell her that wasn't true— but she got mad at me and told me to leave. I thought she was just being a drama queen, so I left her there. I never thought she'd . . ."

His hands are shaking now. "I know I should have called the cops when I heard she was dead, but I was just so scared. I thought they'd blame me or something."

I grab one of his hands and try to keep them still. "Rollins. Trust me. It's going to be okay. But you definitely need to tell the police what you know."

"I know. You're right. I have to tell them." It's like he's trying to convince himself.

"Hey, I'll come with you," I say. "It'll have to be tomorrow, though, because I've got to do this thing for my sister tonight."

"Vee?" He traces a finger on the palm of my hand. "I miss you."

"I miss you, too," I whisper. We sit there for a long moment, electricity flowing from his fingers to mine and then back again.

A knock on my door startles us both, and then my dad calls out, his voice strange. "Vee? You've got another visitor."

I pull my hands away and stand up. "Come in," I reply.

Zane enters the room, confusion clouding his eyes. Even though I haven't done anything wrong, I feel like I have.

"Hey," I say too loudly. "Um, Rollins, I don't think you've officially met Zane. Zane, this is my best friend, Rollins."

Rollins stands. The two eye each other suspiciously. Finally, Zane moves closer and holds out a hand, which Rollins takes grudgingly.

"Rollins was just going," I say abruptly, realizing a second too late how rude it sounds. I want to take the words back, invite Rollins to stay, but he's already moving toward the doorway. He pauses to stand before Zane.

"Be good to her," he says, an undercurrent of threat beneath his words. Before Zane can respond, Rollins disappears out the door. A sadness takes root in my belly. I'm not sure things can ever be the same between Rollins and me—not when Zane's around.

"I'm sorry," I say to Zane, even though I'm not really sure what I'm apologizing for. I just know the scene probably looked pretty fishy to him, and I don't want him to think I have romantic feelings for Rollins. He's just a friend. My best friend in the whole world.

"Don't worry about it," Zane says, wrapping his arms around my waist and nuzzling my hair. "He's protective. I get it. I would be, too."

His lips graze mine.

"Just a second," I say, pulling away and holding up one finger. I push the door closed and then melt into his arms.

———

Tilting my head toward my alarm clock, I see that it's nearly six. I groan, remembering that Samantha Phillips will be here to pick me up in an hour. It almost makes me laugh, to think of myself attending a cheerleader party after all this time.

Zane touches my lips. "What's so funny?"

"Ugh. I have to go this party tonight. It's for my sister. It's her birthday."

A shadow crosses his face. "I thought you said you were worried about Mattie. We were just going to stay home and watch movies."

"I know," I say. "But it's really for the best. She needs to get out of the house. I'll be with her. Nothing will happen. You can come, too, if you want."

He pauses before speaking. "Sure. I'll come. But first could you drop by my house? There's something I want to show you."

"You could show me right now," I say teasingly, but his face remains serious. "Of course I'll come over. I'll have Samantha drop me off, okay? Then you can drive us to the party later."

Zane's face breaks into a smile. He leans over and presses his lips to mine. I sink back against my pillow, getting lost in the moment.

Just then, my door swings open. Startled, Zane and I pull apart. My dad stands in the doorway, looking partly embarrassed but mostly pissed. He clears his throat.

"Sylvia, I think it's about time for your friend to go home."

"God, Dad, how about knocking next time?" I tuck my hair behind my ear and give Zane an *I'm sorry* look.

"It's cool," Zane says, standing quickly, smoothing his clothes. "I should be going anyway." He nods at my father, muttering something about it being nice to meet him, while edging his way out of the room. "See you tonight, Vee."

My father gives me a stern look. "Five minutes. Downstairs."

I groan.

As I stand, I notice a red stain on the carpet near my bed. I kneel down to examine the spot. Unable to rub it out, I realize it's paint. Red paint.

Huh. That's weird.

Before I go down to talk to my father, I get a wet wash-cloth and scrub at the paint. The stain refuses to come out. Vanessa's going to have a shit fit.

———

Whenever we get in trouble, my father summons us to his office. Maybe he thinks this gives him a psychological advantage because it's his turf or something.

I hover in the doorway while he finishes typing. He makes me wait a little bit before acknowledging my presence. Then he gestures for me to sit across from him.

"I guess I haven't made a rule about boys in your bedroom," he says after a long minute. "I haven't really needed to before today."

"You were fine with Rollins coming into my room," I point out.

"Yeah, well, that's Rollins. This boy, Zane—you've never even told me about him. Then he shows up one day out of the blue and I find you two on top of each other?"

Heat rushes into my cheeks. "It's not like that."

"Well, what *is* it like, Sylvia?"

I look away from him. Under his desk, the crumpled photograph of the white-haired woman still sits at the bottom of his trash can. I clench my fists.

"How dare you lecture me about not telling you every little detail in my life? Between you and me, I think you're the one with the most secrets."

His glare falters, just a little, but it's enough for me to

see the crack in his armor. I've found his Achilles' heel, the thing he's been keeping from us all along. Bending down, I retrieve the picture and smooth it out on his desk.

"Would you mind telling me who *this* is?"

His face grows paler by degrees. He stares at the picture beneath my hands like it's something alive, something about to attack him, a wild animal.

"That's—that's all in the past," he says finally.

"*What* is all in the past?"

He squeezes his eyes closed, as if trying to block something out. "My affair." His voice is so small, I have to strain to hear it.

"Your affair? Who'd you have an affair with? This lady?"

He sighs. "Yes. But, Vee, it ended long ago."

I pick up the picture and stare at the white-haired lady in astonishment. This woman was my father's lover?

"When exactly were you with her?" I ask, dreading the answer.

"When you were little," he says softly, confirming what I'd dreaded.

"When Mom was still alive?"

He nods and reaches out, tries to take my hand, but all I see in my head is my mother at home, cancer silently eating her from inside, and him shacking up with the white-haired lady. I stand, still clutching the photograph in my hand. Scrutinizing the picture, I'm struck by the need to know the name of the woman.

"Who is she?"

"Does it matter? It's over now."

"If you've got her picture in your office, it's not over. If she's calling you, it's not over."

He looks baffled. "How did you know she called me?"

"Never mind," I say stubbornly. "What. Is. Her. Name?"

We are in a staring contest. Finally, he looks away. "Evelyn. Evelyn Morrow."

Morrow. I know that name. The name from the tombstone. The name of the little girl who died under my father's knife. He slept with Allison's mother? That doesn't make any sense. Why would he sleep with the mother of one of his patients? To ask him, though, I'd have to explain how I broke into his bottom drawer and looked through his personal papers.

Instead, I say, "Why?" I hate the way my voice sounds, like it's breaking. I hate the weakness, the hurt that coats the simple question.

His face has drained of blood. He looks like I've slapped him.

He doesn't speak.

I slam out of the room.

CHAPTER TWENTY-SIX

I stand in front of Mattie's door, staring at the sparkly My Little Pony stickers she'd decorated it with when she was little. I hear Pearl Jam's "Black" playing in the background again. I pound on the wood with the heel of my hand.

"What do you want?"

"It's almost seven. Are you dressed?"

When Mattie doesn't respond, I push into the room. She's sitting on her bed in her underwear, looking out the window into the dark.

"Is that what you're wearing to Samantha's house?"

She says nothing.

I go to her closet and look over her inventory. She hasn't done laundry in days, just tossed her dirty clothes on the floor. There are only a few shirts, a pair of jeans, and a skirt still on hangers. I pull out a pink long-sleeved T-shirt and jeans and carry them to her bed. On the way, my knees go out and my muscles turn to jelly.

The next thing I know, I'm staring into my own face as my sister hunches over me. I've slid into my sister. I'm seeing everything from her perspective—including my own body. It's completely surreal.

"Vee? Vee? Are you okay?" She shakes my shoulders, and my eyes roll back into my head.

"Oh god. Oh god. I'm sorry. It's my fault. I'll get dressed. I'll go to the party. Just wake up." Tears splash down her cheeks and onto my face. I can't stand to see her like this. I decide to take over, just to calm her down.

Hijacking my sister's body is about as easy as it gets. Maybe it has something to do with genes, but moving her limbs feels natural. I sit back and take a few breaths.

"It's okay," I say, even though I'm not sure she can hear me. I don't feel her there at all anymore, like she's gone to sleep or something. "It's going to be okay. Everything is going to be okay. We're going to go to this party, and we're going to have fun. Just *chill*."

When my sister's muscles have relaxed a bit, I let go of her, will myself to return. I can almost feel the energy channeling out of her and flowing back into my body, only inches away.

I open my eyes to see Mattie sitting calmly by my side. "I don't know what happened," she says, smiling. "But I feel so much better."

———

Samantha pulls into our driveway around 7:05. Mattie jumps into the front seat, and I skulk into the back. Samantha flashes me a totally fake smile, like the past year hasn't happened and we're still besties.

"Can you drop me off at Zane's? He's going to drive me over."

"Zane?" Samantha asks, eyeing me in the backseat.

"Yeah. He lives on Arbor." I pull the seat belt over my lap and click it in. I've seen enough of Samantha's driving to know I'm not really ever safe when she's behind the wheel, even if I'm only riding with her for a few blocks.

"I guess," she says reluctantly, steering the car toward Arbor Lane.

"This is it," I say, pointing.

She pulls into his driveway and barely even waits for me to climb out before she peels backward, into the street. Her car disappears around the corner, and I hear her engine revving as she picks up speed.

I knock on the door, and then stare at an ugly jack-o'-lantern carved to look like a demon. I wonder who carved it—Zane or his mother? Whoever it was has some skill with a knife.

Again, I knock, shifting my weight from one foot to the other. I need to talk to someone about what happened with my father. I need to talk to Zane.

Still, no one answers the door.

He *did* ask me to come over. Surely it wouldn't be that rude to just go in. Maybe the television is on really loud and he can't hear me. Or maybe he's upstairs.

I ring the doorbell and wait.

When no one comes to the door, I put my hand on the knob and give it a little pressure. It slides easily to the right, and the door opens just a crack. I peer in the front entryway, hoping to hear footsteps, someone coming to see who's been knocking all this time.

But no one does.

"Hello?"

Nothing.

I push the door open wider and see something strange. A tall table—the kind you might set your keys or gloves on—is tipped over, a smashed vase on the floor next to it. Shattered glass surrounds a withered rose.

"Hello?"

I step inside, eyeing the mess.

This doesn't look good. I should leave. I *know* I should leave, but something keeps me glued to the floor. I have to find Zane, make sure he's okay.

"Zane?"

I set the table upright and look around. A large open area off to the right seems to be the living room. I think I can make out the shape of a television in the dark. To my left is a staircase. The only light shines down a long hallway directly before me.

My feet carry me toward the light. I find myself in a small kitchen at the end of the hall. A small olive-colored refrigerator stands in the corner, covered with little cow magnets. But most of the room is taken up by a round wooden table.

Every inch of the table is covered in papers. Bills. Junk mail. I recognize a few of Zane's papers from school. In the middle of everything is a small, generic desk calendar. Today's date is circled in red marker.

October 27.

Mattie's birthday.

Déjà vu slams into me. The white page I found on our door on the day Sophie died, on her birthday. The date was circled in red. It was that piece of paper I was holding when I slid into the killer.

My knees slam into the floor.

The paper came from this house.

The paper came from Zane.

Holy shit.

My mind reels as I search for an explanation. There must be some reason for this calendar. I mean, plenty of people must have them. Mr. Golden has one. It's just an ordinary desk calendar.

But not everyone circles dates in red.

I review the past week.

Zane's first day of school was the day Sophie died. Coincidence?

Under the bleachers, Zane rejected my theory that Sophie was murdered. Was he afraid I'd find out the truth?

The red stain on my carpet. Had he been the one to vandalize Mattie's locker? He'd had plenty of time to do it while I was in Mr. Golden's room. The blood-red paint wasn't a prank—it was a threat.

This whole time, I've been so desperate to believe a boy like Zane could ever be drawn to a girl like me. Let's face it—he's amazingly hot. He could have any girl he wanted. Yet *he* approached *me*. Was I too blind to see the real reason? All this time, was he using me to get close to Mattie?

It's *her birthday* that's circled in red. Just like Sophie's.

Oh, shit.

My boyfriend has a bizarre fetish for killing cheerleaders, and he's probably on his way to Samantha's house right this minute. I have to get there first. I have to find Mattie. The only problem is that Sam's house is on the other side of town. I'll never get there in time.

I dig my cell phone out of my pocket and call the only person in this world I can really count on. Rollins picks up on the second ring.

"Vee? What's up?"

"Rollins." I have to fight to make my words understandable because my throat has started to close up. "Rollins, you've got to help me."

"What's wrong?"

"Can you come get me? I'm at Zane's house, on Arbor. Hurry, please. I think something terrible is going to happen." I back out of the kitchen, feeling like I might puke if I look at that stupid calendar any longer.

"Are you okay? What's the address? I'm coming."

"Just hurry. Don't worry about the address. I'll be standing in front."

"I'll be right there."

Over and over, I try to call Mattie, but no one picks up. I bounce up and down, waiting for Rollins to arrive, hoping that the music at the party is just too loud for Mattie to hear her phone ring. Because I can't let myself think about the alternative.

Please. Please just let me get there in time.

―――

"So what's this all about?" Rollins asks, steering toward Samantha's side of town.

I review the events of the last week, trying to think how to distill them into a sentence that will make sense to him. My brain is numb. It refuses to work properly. "I'm just worried about Mattie. I shouldn't have let her go to the party alone."

When we turn onto Samantha's street, we're confronted with a wall of cars.

Rollins grunts in frustration, looking for enough space to park. I squirm, clutching the door handle.

"Just let me out in front. You can meet me inside."

"You sure?" Rollins asks doubtfully, but instead of a response I throw the door open wide and leap out. I steady myself and then run toward Samantha's house. Even if I'd never been here before—which I have, a million times in a past life—it would be easy to tell which house is hers. Every single light is blazing, and music pumps into the night air. There are a couple of senior boys standing on the front porch, slurping lazily from bottles.

"Hey, pinky," the one wearing a football jersey slurs. "Want a beer?"

"Have you seen my sister?" I demand.

He grins. "Your sister? She as cute as you?" He reaches toward me and grabs my shoulder. I snarl at him, and he snatches his hand away. "Okay, okay. Jeez."

I push past them and let myself into Samantha's house. Music reverberates through the walls, more a feeling than a sound. I smell cigarettes and weed and stale beer and body odor.

The foyer is packed wall to wall with drunk kids. I keep my eyes peeled for Mattie, but she's nowhere to be seen. Anxiously, I push past the cheerleaders and jocks doing body shots off each other, into the kitchen, where a couple of idiots are wrestling with a beer bong.

Through the glass door that opens onto the deck, I see a snatch of white T-shirt steal behind a tree. Straining my eyes, I peer through the darkness. A figure dashes out, passing through a pool of light shining from a room upstairs, and in that split second, I recognize him.

Zane.

And he's carrying something.

I pull the door open and step into the chill of the night. The wind rustles the trees and bushes. Zane has disappeared from sight. Slowly, I cross the deck and peer over the side.

"Zane?" I call out uncertainly. "Come out where I can see you."

A figure emerges from behind a tree. It's Zane, his face illuminated by the light coming from behind me. He looks stricken. "Vee? What are you doing here? I thought you were going to my house."

"What are you doing, Zane?" My eyes fall to the red plastic container he's holding.

"You have to get out of here," he says, throwing a nervous look to the bushes behind him. "Vee. You have to run."

"I know what you did, Zane. I was there when you killed Sophie."

A look of confusion crosses Zane's face. Just then, someone else bursts out of the shadows.

It's the white-haired woman.

Evelyn.

I look from Zane to Evelyn and back again. What is my father's mistress doing here? Her face twists in rage, and she begins shouting. "What do you mean, she was going to our house? They were both supposed to be here."

My mind lingers on the words *our house*, and I'm trying to figure out what they mean when a smell, unmistakable and terrifying, rises from below.

Gasoline.

"No matter," Evelyn says. "They're both here now." She waves her arm over her head, and I realize she's holding a book of matches.

An alarm goes off inside me.

For some reason, this crazy woman is going to start a fire.

And Mattie's somewhere inside.

Who *are* these people?

And why are they doing this to us?

I spin around, knowing I have only moments before the woman throws a match on the death trap she and Zane have created. It's not enough time.

I throw open the door and start screaming. It's like I'm in a dream, yelling so loudly, but no one can hear me. They all keep smiling, nodding, dancing, talking, grinding. I push into the crowd, still yelling.

"Get out!" My voice gets sucked up in the sea of bad techno and laughter. "Get out of the house! Fire! Fire! FIRE!"

Finally, people turn toward me, their faces changing, delight melting into fear, their mouths forming Os as they realize what I'm saying. One person after another starts to echo my cry.

"Fire!"

"Get out!"

"Fire!"

One person misinterprets the situation and yells, "Cops!" but it doesn't matter. The effect is the same. Bodies scattering, pushing to get out.

Where is Mattie? Where is she?

I run down the hallway, continuing to scream. It takes all my strength to push past the people coming the other way. In the back room, slumped on a bed, is my sister. She loosely holds a plastic cup, the last dregs of a beer sloshing around inside. How did she get drunk so fast? She's only been here for an hour.

"Mattie! Mattie! Get up! There's a fire!"

Her head lolls to the side. "Vee? Whass goin on? I feel funny."

Smoke tickles my nostrils, threateningly thick.

I muster all my strength and pull her to her feet, adrenaline pumping through me. I practically carry her down the hall to the living room. Thick smoke has filled the room, but I can make out a girl lying on a plaid couch, her legs splayed. It's Samantha.

I can't just leave her here to die, but I can't carry her and my sister at the same time.

I look toward the front door, where the foyer has cleared out. I carry my sister out to the yard. Small groups of people stand around, looking at the house.

Someone is calling my name. I turn around to find Rollins rushing toward me, looking scared out of his skull.

"Christ, Vee. I thought you were still inside."

"Here. Take Mattie. I have to go back." I push Mattie into his arms and turn toward the house, which is being overtaken by flames.

Rollins grabs my arm. "What? No!"

I would be lying if I said there isn't a moment I think about just standing there on the front lawn. The night of the homecoming dance replays in my head, and I think about how Samantha just stood there as Scotch dragged me into the boys' locker room. She didn't do anything. The moment is brief, but it is undeniably there. But I know I would never be able to live with myself if I let Samantha burn.

"Samantha's still inside," I yell, and then bolt back into the house. The air has become so toxic, I start to cough almost immediately. I cover my mouth and nose with my hand to try to filter out some of the smoke.

Samantha is still on the couch. I shake her hard. "Samantha! Wake up!"

But she won't wake up, no matter how hard I shake her. I grab her arms and drag her off the couch. I can barely see my way to the door. Gasping, I take in a mouthful of blackness. The smoke invades my lungs, and I feel myself choking.

Everything goes black.

CHAPTER TWENTY-SEVEN

I'm standing on a dock, at the edge of a lake at the camp I went to when I was little. My dad sent my sister and me here each summer after my mother died. It was cheaper than day care. This place, on the dock, was where I'd come when I got homesick—not for our house, but for Mom.

The only noise now is the lapping of little waves. A peacefulness washes over me. I lower myself until my belly is pressed against the hard wood and I'm able to hang my arm down and tickle the surface of the water with my finger. The lake is so cool, while the rest of my body is hot. So, so hot.

A terrible cough seizes my body, and I crumple into it. My lungs are on fire. My elbows, my toes are on fire. When the cough ceases, I spread out my body, looking at the cloudy sky. I pray for rain to soothe my burning flesh.

Fat drops start falling all around me, bouncing off my skin and streaming onto the dock. I open my mouth, welcoming the moisture with my tongue. The rain soaks my clothes and hair.

"Sylvia." A voice sweet as honey echoes over the water.

It's my mother.

I sit up and look for her. She rows toward me in a red canoe. She guides the oar steadily through the water, first on one side of the boat and then the other. I blink, and she's here, aligning the boat with the side of the dock.

I look into the bottom of the boat and see a nest of blankets and a dark-eyed baby. My mother reaches down and snatches up the child, and then she's suddenly standing beside me on the dock.

"Would you like to hold your sister?" My mother offers the bundle to me, a gentle smile on her face.

"That's not Mattie," I say, unsure of myself.

"No. Your other sister. The one you never got to know."

My other sister? What is she talking about?

I take the child into my arms, and it weighs no more than a small sack of apples.

My mother is staring at me like she's trying to memorize my face. "You could stay here with us if you want." She sweeps her arm, gesturing to the lake, the woods, the never-ending sky.

"What is this place? Heaven?"

She shrugs.

"No offense, Mom, but I didn't like this place much as a kid, and I sure as hell don't want to spend the rest of eternity here."

She smiles. "I understand."

"I have to go back."

"Yes," she agrees. "You still have so much to do."

I start to cry.

My mother comes closer, wraps one arm around me, and rubs my back. I don't move, just soak up the feeling of my mother's hand. The baby coos in my arms.

"You've done well," she says softly.

She pulls her hand away. Even though I want to beg her not to go, I don't. How can I? She's already gone. She eases the baby back into the nest of blankets in the canoe and climbs in, one foot and then the other, carefully balancing her weight so the canoe doesn't tip.

She turns to me and blows me a kiss.

And then, she's gone.

———

Sirens blare in the distance, growing ever closer. The grass is cold beneath me. I roll to the side and cough until my throat is raw. Someone is stroking my hair the whole time. Foolishly, I believe for a moment that it could be my mother.

I open an eye and see Samantha's body lying nearby on the lawn. A few cheerleaders are leaning over her, holding her hand and crying.

"Vee. Say something."

I roll over and look up to see Rollins, upside down, staring at me with wild eyes.

"Is Samantha dead?"

He shakes his head. "No. Just unconscious. The paramedics are on their way."

"How did we get out?"

Rollins looks down. "I—I went in after you."

I suck in a deep breath and push myself into a sitting position so my words have full impact. "Do you know how stupid that was?"

Rollins smirks. "Isn't that a little like the pot calling the kettle black?" His face becomes serious. "Vee, don't you ever do anything like that again. I thought . . . I thought . . . Jesus, Vee, don't you know how I feel about you?"

I look away. I think I do know how he feels about me. I think it's something we've been dancing around, ever since homecoming last year. Maybe I've been hiding from it, unwilling to explore a connection that was forged under such disturbing circumstances, but there's no denying there's something there. Still, these are feelings I can't deal with at this moment, not while I'm lying on the cold grass after my so-called boyfriend just tried to kill my sister and a houseful of other people as an afterthought.

Speaking of which—where the hell did Zane go? And Evelyn?

What did Evelyn say before she lit the match?

Our house. Our house. Our house.

The words march through my head.

When it dawns on me, I feel like I'm going to be sick. Evelyn, my father's old lover, is Zane's mother. Allison Morrow must have been Zane's younger sister, the one who died when he was so little.

She was sick. She needed my father to save her, but he wasn't able to. And so Allison died, and Evelyn went crazy.

She yelled at Zane for trying to protect me.

She was trying to kill us.

Me and Mattie.

To get back at my father.

I feel the bile rise in my throat.

Where is Mattie? I scan the lawn quickly but don't see her anywhere.

"Rollins, where's Mattie?"

He looks shaken. "I left her right here to go in after you. I'm sure she didn't go far."

Rollins helps me to stand, and we walk the perimeter of the yard. A few people remain, but it seems most of the partygoers took off when they heard the sirens. A fire truck races down the street and stops in front of Samantha's house. A couple of men wearing thick yellow coats jump down and start unloading equipment.

I grab one of the weepy cheerleaders and ask her if she's seen Mattie. She shakes her head and turns back to Samantha.

I turn to Rollins and speak quickly. "Rollins, you have to take me back to Zane's house. There's no time. Just trust me. We have to go back."

Rollins looks at me, confused, but nods. "Okay. Let's go."

———

On the way to Zane's house, I clutch the sides of my seat. Could Evelyn and Zane have snatched Mattie in her wasted state? Mattie would probably just go with Zane if he said I'd asked him to give her a ride home.

I have no way of knowing where they took her, but I do have the power to find them. If I can find something at their house, something significant to Zane, I can slide into him—hopefully before anything happens to Mattie. Wrapping my arms around myself, I try not to imagine what she could be going through this very second.

After what seems like an eternity, Rollins pulls into Zane's driveway and slams on the brakes. The house looks just as I left it, the front door standing open and light from the kitchen pouring onto the front lawn.

"Come on," I say, climbing out of the car and running to the house. Rollins is close behind me. Once inside, I point out the shattered vase to Rollins. "Watch out."

I climb the staircase, two steps at a time, and pause at the top. There's a short hallway, with two doors on the left and two on the right. I try the first one on the right, but it's only a bathroom.

I try the next door. Jackpot. A narrow bed with black sheets is pushed up against a wall lined with Nirvana posters. Zane's clothes are strewn about, along with some comic books. On his bedside table is his copy of *Tender Is the Night*. Bingo. It has to lead me to him. It has to.

"Okay," I say, turning to Rollins. "This is it. You just have to trust me on this. I'm going to make myself pass out. You just stay here with me, okay? If anyone comes home, shake me until I wake up. Will you do that?"

Rollins shrugs. "What choice are you giving me?"

"None," I reply. I grab the novel, the pages soft and worn from constant handling, and I lie back on Zane's bed. "Remember, if anyone comes, wake me up." With that, I clutch the book and squeeze my eyes closed. For a long, terrifying moment, I'm afraid it's not going to work.

I realize I'm too amped-up to slide. My pulse is racing, and I can't stop picturing what might be happening to

Mattie this very second. Forcing myself to breathe deeply and slowly, I try to relax all my muscles. Rollins runs his hand through my hair, and that makes all the difference. I feel myself get drowsy.

And then the dizziness sets in, and the pain.

———

Black road stretches out before me. Broken bits of a yellow line disappear under the dashboard, racing under the car. Zane is on the passenger side, clutching the plastic container. The reek of gasoline makes me feel sick.

Evelyn is driving. Mattie is nowhere to be seen, I realize with relief.

Zane opens his mouth to speak. His voice is all wobbly and broken. I realize he's crying. "You didn't have to hurt her," he says. "Mattie would have been enough to get back at him."

"Dammit, Zane," the woman spits out, throwing a glare at him. "Don't you care about your little sister at all? First you try to warn them by pulling that ridiculous prank at the high school, and then you try to save that miserable Sylvia. I can't believe you. These are the people who destroyed Allison. If those girls didn't exist, your sister would still be alive. But no. Jared had to protect his precious little family, even if it meant shattering ours."

"But that girl, Sophie, had nothing to do with what happened to Allison." Zane is shaking. His grip on the jug of gasoline loosens, and I realize how stupid it is to be carrying such a thing inside a moving vehicle.

Evelyn sharpens her words, flings them at him like knives. "Nothing to do with her? You've got to be kidding me. She was born the very same day Allison died. I remember that day so well. I was sitting in the waiting room when the nurse came out to tell me my baby was dead. And Sophie's family was whooping it up with balloons and champagne. Can you tell me that's fair?"

Zane shifts the jug of gas from one knee to the other. "But the other girl, Amber. She did nothing to you."

His mother sneers. "I didn't kill her. She must have killed herself. There's something contagious about suicide, isn't there? One person goes, and it's like a domino effect."

Zane stares at his mother. "You're crazy. I should have gone to the police when I had the chance."

She slaps him in the back of the head. "How dare you call your own mother insane? Do you think I wouldn't do the same thing if someone hurt you? That's what being a mother is about. Protecting your children."

"You haven't protected me," Zane says. "You ruined me. You made my whole life about revenge. You filled my head with lies about a killer surgeon and his spoiled daughters. But you were wrong, Mother. You were *wrong*."

Evelyn stares at her son as if he's speaking another language. Zane turns his head toward the dashboard, and I feel his eyes widen in panic. Evelyn doesn't see the way the road twists suddenly to the left. Zane grabs for the wheel, but it's too late. The car shoots off the road, straight toward a tree.

The last thing I hear is Zane's scream.

And I realize it's coming from me.

CHAPTER TWENTY-EIGHT

Someone is shaking me.

"Vee? Vee!"

Rollins.

"I'm here. I'm okay," I reassure him, blinking in the sudden light of Zane's room. My head is on Rollins's lap, and his hands are cupping my face. He looks scared. I push away from him unsteadily.

Zane's scream is still ringing in my ears. I feel like I'm going to vomit.

I try to stand, but all the strength has left my legs. Rollins helps me to my feet. My hands are all rubbery, but I shove them into my pocket, searching for my cell phone. Fumbling, I pull it out, scroll down to my sister's number, and hit the Call button. The phone rings once, twice, three times . . . but no one picks up. I quickly dial our home phone number.

My dad picks up on the second ring, his voice breathless.

"Dad. Is Mattie there?"

"Where are you, Vee? I've been worried. I was afraid you were stuck in that house—"

"I'm fine. Mattie's there?" I interrupt.

"Yes. One of her friends drove her home. She's three sheets to the wind, but she's alive. Thank god. Are you on your way home?"

"Yes," I say, holding on to Rollins's sleeves for support. "I'm coming home right now."

I hang up and put the phone away.

"She's okay?" Rollins asks.

"Yes," I say. "Can you give me a ride? I just want to go home."

"Of course," he says, sounding bewildered.

I take a step toward the doorway and stumble, but Rollins stabilizes me.

"Easy," he says. "Vee, you're going to tell me what this is all about, right?"

I grab his hand and squeeze. "Yes. I promise."

He hooks an arm under my armpit. He helps me down the stairs, guides me past the broken glass, and tucks me into his car. Inside, it's warm and safe. I'm reminded of the night of the homecoming dance last year, when he rescued me from Scotch's probing hands. Just like that night, Rollins drives me home.

———

I lie on my bed, watching headlights from passing cars shine on my ceiling. No matter how hard I try, I can't get the sound of the crash out of my head. Zane's and his mother's shrieks, laced together for all eternity.

I called 911 to report the crash as soon as I got home,

as soon as it occurred to me. The operator said an ambulance was already on the scene. I asked if everyone was okay, but she couldn't give me any details. She suggested I call the hospital, but when I did, they said they couldn't give out information.

My alarm clock blinks away the minutes, stretching them out into forever. For the first time since my mother died, I pray. I pray for Zane's life. I pray for justice—whether that means his mother's death or consecutive lifetime prison sentences, I don't know. I'll leave that up to the powers that be.

I pray for morning.

———

When the doorbell rings, my father is in the kitchen flipping chocolate-chip pancakes. Mattie's still asleep. Only I am left to see who it is. I pad to the front entryway in my slippers and peek through the curtain. Officer Teahen is standing there, hands thrust in his pockets, head tilted up toward the sky. I pull open the door.

"Officer Teahen," I say. "Can I help you with something?"

"Uh, Mattie?" He squints his eyes at me, like my name might be etched into my forehead somewhere.

"No, I'm Sylvia," I say.

"Is your father around?"

I nod, staring at him with wide eyes. After taking a few deep breaths, I call for my dad. He appears, wiping his hands on a dish towel.

"Officer Teahen." My father's voice is hard. "What can I do for you?"

Melting into the background, I sit on the stairs. I read a hundred different intentions in the officer's eyes. Zane and his mother are dead. The police found my fingerprints in their house and want to question me about what happened. Or they traced the 911 call and want to know how I knew about the crash. Or Zane and his mother are alive and Zane's mother wants my father arrested for "killing her baby" so many years ago.

The officer nods at my father and says, "Mr. Bell. I have some questions for you regarding a woman named Evelyn Morrow."

My father glances in my direction, then steps onto the front porch and closes the door. He doesn't return for a long time. When he does, his eyes are bloodshot and weepy-looking. He never looks like this. Never. He comes toward me, his arms stretched out like a zombie's. I don't understand what he's doing until he reaches me and hugs me until I can't breathe. But I don't want him to stop. I don't want him to let go.

"I'm so sorry, Vee," he says, stroking my hair, and that's when I know it's over. Zane is dead. I was stupid to ever think differently. Stupid to hope. I am stupid. So stupid.

My father pulls back and looks me in the face. "Zane has been in a car accident. Honey, I'm so sorry. Zane is dead."

That's when I collapse.

———

I awake to my father's voice.

"Vee. Wake up. Sylvia."

I open an eye and realize I'm lying on the wooden floor. For a moment, I think this must be what it feels like to lie in a coffin, everything cold and hard.

Wrenching my head to the right, I throw up. My father holds my hair.

"That's okay, VeeVee. Let's go upstairs and get you cleaned up. Do you think you can stand?" my father asks when I'm done puking. I don't think I can. In fact, I'm pretty sure I'll never stand again. But I plant my feet on the floor and wrap my arms around his neck and—lo and behold—I'm standing. Upstairs we go, one foot in front of the other, and then down the hall to the bathroom.

My father holds his hand under the faucet until the water is just right and then helps me to undress. He looks away the whole time. And I think about Rollins and his mother and how this is just what you do for someone you love when they can't do it for themselves.

After my bath, my father helps me into my room. I let him pile the covers on top of me. He pulls the blinds tight and leaves. My eyes are wide open.

Hours pass.

I do not sleep.

———

Late that night, I give up on sleep and turn on my light. My bookshelf glows like it's beckoning to me. I kneel before it, looking for the book he spoke of, the one he made me promise to read again—under a tree, at dusk. My fingertips find it before my eyes do.

The Great Gatsby.

I steal down the stairs, grab my jacket from its hook and a flashlight from the junk drawer. Careful not to make too much noise, I ease the back door open ever so carefully until the gap is just wide enough for me to slip through.

The night is cold, but I welcome it. I need to feel something other than loss, something other than pain. There is only one tree in our backyard, a great big oak tree, but it's perfect. I settle down beneath it and crack the spine on my book. It's not dusk, but it will have to do.

Just like Zane said, the experience is totally different. I'm not reading to pass a stupid English quiz. I'm reading for my life, for what Zane's life was. I'm reading to see the book through his eyes. At first, the pages move slowly, but before I know it I'm halfway through the book.

Soon, it is light, and the book is done. It swallowed me whole and then released me, a different person than I was before. I lie back and watch the sun inching its way upward. Maybe I didn't ever really know Zane, but on the other hand—maybe the part he showed to me was the only part of him that was real. I lie there until the sun stings my eyes, and then I pick myself up off the lawn.

CHAPTER TWENTY-NINE

My father stands in the kitchen, layering noodles on top of Italian sausage, mozzarella, and spinach. Mattie is sitting at the dining room table in front of her laptop. It is a familiar scene, but nothing about it feels right. Now that I know my father has been lying to us all these years—not only about having an affair, but also about having another *daughter*, I've been careful around him. Polite, but not overly warm.

I've decided I can't let us go on like this, living a lie. It would have been better if this was his idea, but I'm tired of waiting. I need to get things out in the open, set everything straight. So I slide onto a stool across from him. The framed picture of my mother is heavy in my lap.

"Dad? I need to talk to you about something."

He must see the seriousness in my eyes because he puts down the bag of cheese and leans forward. "What is it, Vee?"

I hold up the picture. I remove the back, retrieve the key, and lay it gently on the counter. "What's this?"

His voice is calm, and he looks me right in the eyes.

"The key to my desk. I hide it because there are important documents in there, things like your birth certificate."

"Is that all that's in there?"

My sister has stopped goofing around on the computer and is staring at us.

My dad's eyes drop, can't sustain the gaze. When he looks back up at me, his eyes are full of tears. "I know it's time to tell you. I just got used to being the hero, though, you know? The man who saves babies and comes home to his beautiful daughters. Because after I tell you this, I don't know if you'll feel the same way about me."

"What are you talking about, Dad?" Mattie leaves her place at the dining room table and moves to sit next to me on one of the stools.

I steel myself. "Go on."

"I'm guessing you already looked in the drawer. You saw the medical records." He directs his words to me.

I nod.

"What's going on? What drawer?" Mattie asks.

My father takes a deep breath. "I had an affair, Mattie. Years ago, when your mother was still alive. Vee was just a toddler. Your mother was pregnant with you."

Mattie looks stricken. "You slept with someone? When Mom was pregnant?"

He looks at his hands, covered in marinara. He's clearly miserable. I almost feel sorry for him. But we need to get this over with.

"Yes. We had a fight. She was angry that I was working such long hours. She accused me of having an affair. I thought . . . I thought maybe I should just have one, since she thought that anyway."

Mattie covers her mouth with her hand. I reach over and gently rub her back. I know how shocked I was when I found out. It must be even worse for her, on top of everything she's been through lately.

"It was just the one time. But it was enough. Those medical records that you saw, Vee. The ones for Allison Morrow? She was my daughter. Your sister. She was born prematurely with a severe malformation. I was the only one who could help her. I tried. . ."

When he breaks up into sobs, I feel horrible. No matter what he did, he's my father, and he lost someone he loved, just like I lost Mom. Seeing him so emotional tears me up inside.

"I did everything I could do," he whispers, wiping away tears with fingers that leave tomato sauce on his cheeks. "I tried to save her."

I don't say anything for a moment. The only sound is my father and sister crying. It's almost finished. I just need to know one more thing.

"Zane," I say quietly.

"Yes," he says, grabbing a paper towel and wiping his face. "Zane was her son."

"Why didn't you tell me? Especially when you found out we were together?"

"I—I couldn't. I wasn't ready. Evelyn started calling me, and I froze. Didn't know what to do." I try to digest this news, that Evelyn was stalking my father. He continues on. "You can't know the guilt I've felt for these last fourteen years, Vee.

It's what I think about when I get up in the morning, when I look in the mirror. I think about it every time I scrub in to operate on another baby, someone else's baby."

I can't even fathom it, not being able to save your own daughter. Some things are too horrific to imagine, and coming from me, that's huge.

Tracing my fingers over my mother's portrait, I try to picture my dad snuggled in bed next to me and my mother, Mattie in her belly. Does the fact that my father slept with another woman take away the fact that he loved us so much? That he would have done anything for my mother? Does it take away the years he's spent taking care of us?

I look back at him, and I see my father for what he is.

A man.

He is just a man. One night, he drank a little too much and did something stupid. He made a mistake. But he is more than that mistake. He is the man who makes us lasagna, the man who holds my mother's picture and cries when he thinks no one is looking, the man who makes broken babies whole.

He is just a man. But he is a good man.

"Can you girls ever forgive me?" he asks, not daring to look up.

I climb off the stool, walk around the counter, and put my arm around him.

"Yes," I say simply.

Mattie follows my lead and tucks herself beneath his other arm. "Yes," she says.

We stand there, together, the three of us.

A family.

Marty's Diner is dead for a Sunday morning. A couple of waitresses lean against the counter, talking about the woman and boy who died in a car crash a week ago. It's been all over the news, how the cops went to the lady's house and found evidence in the basement—guns, rope, gasoline. There was also a diary filled with her mad ravings about how Jared Bell killed her baby and how she was going to get back at our family and also pretty much every kid in Mattie's grade. It was her intention to kill everyone at Samantha's party, a chubby waitress says. The tall one shakes her head, unbelieving.

Rollins sits across from me in the booth, watching me play with sugar packets.

"Vee. I'm really sorry about Zane."

I am silent.

He tries again. "I mean, I wasn't his biggest fan, but the important thing was that he made you happy. I'm sure he was a good guy. You know, despite the fact his mom was crazy."

I try to make a little house with the packets, but it keeps falling down. I give up.

"I do want you to be happy," he says, putting his hand over mine and the scattered sugar packets.

"I know you do," I say, finally meeting his eyes. "I've been awful the last couple of weeks. There's been so much crap going on . . . but I'm sorry for being a bitch."

He taps my hand with his forefinger. "I'll forgive you if you explain to me what happened that night in Zane's room."

I sigh. I've been dreading this moment, knowing it was just around the corner but hoping I could put it off for a few more days. Today is as good as any, though.

"Okay."

I think for a minute, search for the right words.

"I'm going to tell you something about me, and it's going to sound freaking insane."

He bobs his head encouragingly. "Go on."

"Well, you know how I'm really careful about touching stuff that's not mine?"

Rollins laughs. "You mean your OCD? Yeah, I know."

"It's not OCD, Rollins. It's not narcolepsy, either. It's something else. Something I don't understand. What happens to me when I pass out—it's not right. I told my father about it when it startd, and he sent me to a psychiatrist. So I don't tell people about it anymore, even though it still happens to me."

"What happens?" he asks gently.

I take the leap. "I leave my body. I slide into other people's heads. I see what they see."

Stopping for a moment, I search his eyes for that look, the one my father gave me when I told him, the mixture of fear and disbelief. But there's a different look on Rollins's face entirely. He looks concerned.

"What do you see?"

"It depends. I'll slide into Mr. Nast and see him sneaking drinks of vodka out of a flask. I'll slide into my father and witness an operation. I'll slide into Mattie and see her crying at night. It's different with every person. Mostly I see things I don't want to see."

"Like what?" he prods. There's no mocking in his

tone. He honestly wants to know.

So I tell him. I tell him about Amber and the naked picture of Sophie she sent to all the football players. I tell him about Mr. Golden's affair with Amber's mom. I tell him about witnessing Sophie's death. I tell him about finding out Zane's mother was responsible for everything. I tell him about my last moments with Zane.

Rollins slips out of his side of the booth and scoots in next to me. He puts his arm around me, and I can smell soap under the muskiness of his leather jacket.

"I'm so sorry," he whispers to me.

"I'm okay," I reply. "I'm okay."

It becomes apparent that the waitresses, bored, are staring at us. I nod in their direction. "Rollins, why don't you go back to your side of the table. We're turning into their entertainment."

He gives me one last squeeze and returns to his side.

Ripping open a sugar packet, he says, "So. Did you ever slide into me?" He dumps the contents in his mouth.

Shit.

The one part I left out. I know how he'll feel if he learns I saw his home life. His mother. The things he has to do to take care of her.

The fact that I don't respond tips him off. He'd been joking before, but now he's somber. "You did. Didn't you? When did you slide into me?"

"Last week," I say, squirming. It's suddenly very hot in here.

"Last week? What did you see?"

I shrug off my jacket. I don't know how to tell him I saw his mother naked, how I saw him giving her a bath. I'm boiling with embarrassment.

"Vee. Answer me."

"I saw your house and your uncle and your mother. And I know that you have to help your mom do things, like take baths."

His face is white. "You saw me . . . bathing her?"

"It's okay, Rollins. I know what it's like to take care of someone."

"Stop," he says. "You don't know. You've never had to give your sister or your father a bath. You can't possibly know what it's like. Every day. To be responsible for her well-being every single day. I have to feed her. I have to dress her. There's no one else. Just me."

I don't know what to say. "I'm . . . sorry, Rollins."

He puts his head in his hands. "I can't believe you saw me giving her a bath. I feel like . . . I feel like you *violated* me."

I reach for his hand. "Rollins . . ."

He pulls away. "No. Just leave me alone."

He rises and heads for the door. As I watch him leave, I can't help but feel guilty. He's right. I did violate him. I didn't mean to, but I did. People have a right to their secrets. The fact that I can't help sliding is no excuse.

I remember how it felt to realize Scotch was using my body without my permission. It makes me sick to think about Rollins feeling that same way. Watching Rollins drive away, I try to think of some way to make it up to him.

CHAPTER THIRTY

That night, I peer through my telescope, wondering why the sky looks the same when the universe has been turned completely upside down.

"Vee," my sister says. I turn to see her hovering near my doorway.

"Yes?"

She takes a few steps into my room and lowers herself into the rocking chair. She draws her knees up to her chin and looks at me thoughtfully. "Are you going to be okay?"

I look out the window again, searching. First I see Polaris, shining bright. From there, I make out Ursa Minor, the baby bear. Close by, as always, is Ursa Major. The mother bear.

"Yeah," I say. "I'll be fine. Just give me a while."

"Do you want to talk about him?"

"Who? Zane?" I turn back toward my sister.

"Yeah, tell me about him." She cocks her head to the side, the way she used to when I read her stories before bedtime.

I climb onto my bed and think awhile.

Finally, I speak. "He wasn't afraid. He'd gone through so much pain in his life, but he didn't hide himself away. Even though he knew how fragile life was—maybe *because* he knew—he seized every moment and made it his own."

She is quiet, as though she's digesting my words.

"Did you love him?"

I have to think about this for a minute. When Zane told me he was falling for me, I was kind of paralyzed. I was so afraid to admit that I loved him, even to myself, because that would mean it would all come to an end and I'd get hurt.

And that's what happened. When I found out who he was, that he'd known what his mother was doing all along, that he was just going to let Mattie die . . .

I got hurt.

Badly.

But that doesn't take away the fact that I cared for him. If only for a little while.

"Yeah. I think I did."

Mattie sighs.

We both sit quietly for a few moments.

"What happened to Rollins?"

I fluff my pillow and lean back on it. "We got into a fight. Just dumb stuff."

"You know he's in love with you, right?"

I pause.

"Yes," I finally admit. "I know."

"You should make up with him. He's a good guy." Mattie's voice is soft, and she reminds me of how she used to be as a child. Sweet. Kind.

"Maybe we will," I say, but only to appease her. Rollins has been keeping his secrets so long. I have a feeling it's going to take a while for him to forgive me for what I know.

"Hey," I say, pulling myself up. "Do you want to learn how to use Mom's telescope?"

"Sure," she replies, grinning.

I show her how to adjust the lens. She bends over and peers into the telescope, squeezing one eye shut. I watch her for a little while, noticing how she looks kind of like Dad when she's concentrating on something. She's grown up so much in the past week. Her expression is more mature. More adult. I think maybe I should tell her about my sliding sometime. Not tonight, but soon.

When my sister leaves, I lie down on my bed and stare at the ceiling, thinking about what she said—how Rollins is in love with me. I don't know that I have much to offer him right now. But one thing is for sure.

I don't want to lose him as a friend.

I turn over on my side and reach down to my backpack and pull out a notebook and pen. I flip open to a new page. I chew on my pen for a minute, waiting for the words to come to me. When they do, it's in a flood, and I have to chase them with my pen, hurrying to get them all down before they escape.

Dear Rollins,

Since our fight, I've been thinking a lot. I thought I'd take a page from your book and write it all down. I understand why you're upset, and I don't blame you. I'd be angry, too, if someone invaded my privacy like that. Still, I wish you'd been able to share your home life with me. There's so much shit in life—what good are friends if not to help shoulder some of the burden? I guess what I'm saying is, I want you to let me be here for you. I've gotten a taste of what life is like without you as a friend, and I don't want to go back to that. I miss you. So. Much. I hope, once you cool off a little, you'll come around again.

Vee

I rip the page out, fold it half, and stuff it into my backpack. My breath has quickened with the exhilaration of putting myself out there. It feels good. I'm not used to being so bold, but I'm proud of myself for reaching out to Rollins. It's a little scary, I must admit—who's to say Rollins won't sneer at my heartfelt letter, crumple it up, and throw it in the trash?

But maybe he won't.

EPILOGUE

Mattie and I decide our new Friday-night tradition will involve board games and pepperoni pizza. Even Dad gets in on the action, after he finishes complaining that Pizza Hut can't hold a candle to his homemade Chicago-style pizza.

"Where did you get all those twenties?" Mattie asks my father in a whiny voice. "I don't think you should be the banker anymore."

I laugh, pushing my newly blond hair away from my face. Something about the transition back to my natural color just made sense. I am tired of running away from who I am. I'm ready to embrace all of me, good or bad.

I have just purchased Park Place when the doorbell rings. I toss the dice to my sister, who misses them and has to crawl under the table to find them.

"I'll get it," I say, rising and stretching.

I am still smiling when I pull open the door.

He stands there like he belongs on my front porch.

He stands there like he used to.

His hands are behind his back.

"Choose," he says.

"I've already made my choice," I say, and I grab the sleeve of his leather jacket and pull him inside.